SpringerBriefs in Population Studies

Population Studies of Japan

The world population is expected to expand by 39.4% to 9.6 billion in 2060 (UN World Population Prospects, revised 2010). Meanwhile, Japan is expected to see its population contract by nearly one third to 86.7 million, and its proportion of the elderly (65 years of age and over) will account for no less than 39.9% (National Institute of Population and Social Security Research in Japan, Population Projections for Japan 2012). Japan has entered the post-demographic transitional phase and will be the fastest-shrinking country in the world, followed by former Eastern bloc nations, leading other Asian countries that are experiencing drastic changes.

A declining population that is rapidly aging impacts a country's economic growth, labor market, pensions, taxation, health care, and housing. The social structure and geographical distribution in the country will drastically change, and short-term as well as long-term solutions for economic and social consequences of this trend will be required.

This series aims to draw attention to Japan's entering the post-demographic transition phase and to present cutting-edge research in Japanese population studies. It will include compact monographs under the editorial supervision of the Population Association of Japan (PAJ).

The PAJ was established in 1948 and organizes researchers with a wide range of interests in population studies of Japan. The major fields are (1) population structure and aging; (2) migration, urbanization, and distribution; (3) fertility; (4) mortality and morbidity; (5) nuptiality, family, and households; (6) labor force and unemployment; (7) population projection and population policy (including family planning); and (8) historical demography. Since 1978, the PAJ has been publishing the academic journal *Jinkogaku Kenkyu* (The Journal of Population Studies), in which most of the articles are written in Japanese.

Thus, the scope of this series spans the entire field of population issues in Japan, impacts on socioeconomic change, and implications for policy measures. It includes population aging, fertility and family formation, household structures, population health, mortality, human geography and regional population, and comparative studies with other countries.

This series will be of great interest to a wide range of researchers in other countries confronting a post-demographic transition stage, demographers, population geographers, sociologists, economists, political scientists, health researchers, and practitioners across a broad spectrum of social sciences.

Shigeki Matsuda · Hirohisa Takenoshita
Editors

Changes in Work and Family Life in Japan Under COVID-19

Springer

Editors
Shigeki Matsuda
School of Contemporary Sociology
Chukyo University
Toyota-shi, Aichi, Japan

Hirohisa Takenoshita
Faculty of Law
Keio University
Minato-ku, Tokyo, Japan

ISSN 2211-3215 ISSN 2211-3223 (electronic)
SpringerBriefs in Population Studies
ISSN 2198-2724 ISSN 2198-2732 (electronic)
Population Studies of Japan
ISBN 978-981-99-5849-8 ISBN 978-981-99-5850-4 (eBook)
https://doi.org/10.1007/978-981-99-5850-4

This Springer imprint is published by the registered company Springer Nature Singapore Pte Ltd.
The registered company address is: 152 Beach Road, #21-01/04 Gateway East, Singapore 189721, Singapore

Paper in this product is recyclable.

Contents

1 **Impact of the COVID-19 Pandemic on Japanese Society** 1
Shigeki Matsuda

2 **How Does Telework Contribute to Generating Inequality During the COVID-19 Pandemic? The New Origin of Inequality in Japan** 15
JaeYoul Shin and Hirohisa Takenoshita

3 **Impact of the COVID-19 Pandemic on the Gender Gap in Domestic Labor: Evidence from a Two-Wave Survey in Japan** ... 53
Junko Nishimura, Jihey Bae, and Kota Toma

4 **The Impact of the COVID-19 on Fertility in Eastern Asia: The Case of Japan** 85
Nancy L. S. Leung, Takayuki Sasaki, and Shigeki Matsuda

Conclusion 111

Contributors

Jihey Bae J.F. Oberlin University, Tokyo, Japan

Nancy L. S. Leung Nippon Sport Science University, Tokyo, Japan

Shigeki Matsuda Chukyo University, Nagoya, Japan

Junko Nishimura Ochanomizu University, Tokyo, Japan

Takayuki Sasaki Tsuda University, Tokyo, Japan

JaeYoul Shin Hiroshima University, Higashi-Hiroshima, Japan

Hirohisa Takenoshita Keio University, Tokyo, Japan

Kota Toma Kyoto University, Kyoto, Japan

Chapter 1
Impact of the COVID-19 Pandemic on Japanese Society

Shigeki Matsuda

Abstract Since 2020, the COVID-19 pandemic has caused enormous damage worldwide. The virus was detected in Japan in the spring of the same year, and various measures were implemented to prevent its spread, including the declaration of a state of emergency. Unlike emergencies declared by major European countries with strong measures of city-wide lockdowns, Japan's *state of emergency* did not entail coercive force, but was a *request* to people and corporations by the government. These measures have been successful, keeping Japan's COVID-19 human damage at a considerably lower level compared to major Western countries. However, Japan continued its infection control measures indefinitely, while major Western countries later eased and changed their policies to "*with corona*". As a result, the pandemic has not only had a huge impact on Japan's macroeconomy, but also on the work and family life of individuals.

Keywords COVID-19 · Pandemic · State of emergency · Economy · Work and family life

1.1 Occurrence of the COVID-19 Pandemic

The novel coronavirus infection was first identified in December 2019, and the World Health Organization (WHO) declared a Public Health Emergency of International Concern at the end of January 2020. In March, the coronavirus outbreak was considered a pandemic due to its global spread and severity (NIID, 2020). The COVID-19 pandemic devastated several countries around the world; approximately 580 million people infected, and the total death toll reached some 6.4 million at the end of July 2022 (WHO, 2020). To prevent its spread, each country implemented various measures, such as restrictions on movement across countries and regions, restrictions on the operation of restaurants and other establishments, and the promotion of telework. Although there are differences between countries, in general, Western

S. Matsuda (✉)
Chukyo University, Nagoya, Japan
e-mail: matsuda_z113@yahoo.co.jp

S. Matsuda and H. Takenoshita (eds.), *Changes in Work and Family Life in Japan Under COVID-19*, Population Studies of Japan, https://doi.org/10.1007/978-981-99-5850-4_1

countries (especially Western Europe), where the spread of infection was particularly remarkable, implemented strong countermeasures, such as lockdowns in major cities. This greatly impacted countries' economic activities and people's lives.

The pandemic also had a huge social and economic impact on Japan, which is located next to China, the pandemic's epicenter. Japan has dealt with new influenza strain epidemics in the past, but this was its first experience in dealing with a stronger and unidentified infection. At first glance, it seems easier to prevent epidemics in Japan as an island nation, by restricting air and sea routes, and implementing strong quarantine measures, than in countries connected by land. In fact, Japan experienced a symbolic event in January 2020: an overseas luxury liner had a coronavirus outbreak on board. It was dealt with by appropriate quarantine measures while the ship was anchored at Yokohama port, near the Tokyo metropolitan area. This event brought home the serious danger of the pandemic to the Japanese people. However, in the present age of economic globalization, it was difficult for Japan to completely restrict people's immigration. Although the virus's invasion into the country was delayed, eventually the infection spread within the country. While the situation of COVID-19 in Japan, and the countermeasures against it taken by the Japanese government were moderate compared to major Western countries, various social and economic activities were restricted. As such, it had a great impact on individual work and family life, as well as family formation.

In 2022, at the time of writing this chapter, Japan's society and economy have largely returned to their pre-COVID-19 conditions, but the countermeasures are still continuing, albeit in a somewhat relaxed manner. COVID-19 is still classified as category 2 among infectious diseases, the same as Ebola hemorrhagic fever (for reference, seasonal influenza is classified as category 5). Advanced medical care is provided to affected patients, while infected individuals and those in close contact with them, especially through co-living, must stay home for a certain period to prevent spreading of the infection. The total number of infected people is reported daily. The door to Japan from overseas is partially open, and the number of foreigners entering the country is capped per day. Many countries may find it incredulous, but everyone in Japan has worn a mask since the outbreak, even in summer. Japan's policies may seem strange for countries changing their policies to with COVID-19. However, similar situations can be found in various East Asian countries, including China, which had also implemented strong countermeasures, such as locking down certain of its large cities in the summer of 2022.

The purpose of this book is to describe the actual impact of the COVID-19 pandemic on Japanese work and family life between 2020 and 2021, based on official documents and our original surveys. The specific analytical issues discussed in this book primarily belong to three domains: employment and telework, family life (especially sharing domestic chores), and childbirth. The academic contribution made by this book is presenting a cohesive picture of the pandemic's impact on these domains in Japan. Our analysis sheds light on Japan's problems within these domains, while revealing the country's unique situation differing from those of Western and other Asian countries. It is believed that Japan's experience under the pandemic can provide suggestions for future pandemic responses.

1.2 Japan's Infection Status and COVID-19 Countermeasures

Since the onset of the pandemic, the coronavirus has mutated many times, creating multiple waves of infections around the world. Japan also experienced several waves of the virus's spread and convergence. Figure 1.1 shows the specific changes in Japan's COVID-19 infection status. When looking at this Fig. 1.1, it is necessary to keep in mind that Japan's total population is 126 million. The country's first observed case of COVID-19 was in mid-January 2020, with the count for new infections per day reaching a low level of double digits until mid-March. However, the infection spread rapidly after that, with the number of cases per day peaking at over 600 during the first wave of infections occurring in mid-April. The second wave occurred from July to August of the same year, when the Tokyo Olympics were originally scheduled to be held. The peak at this time exceeded 1,000 cases per day. The third wave occurred around the year-end and New Year holidays, when the number of new infections peaked at around 8,000 per day. April–May 2021 saw the fourth wave around the *Golden Week*, a period of consecutive national holidays in May, with more than 7000 cases observed at the peak. At the time of the Tokyo Olympics, the fifth wave peaked in July–September 2021, with 25,000 or more cases, while the sixth wave peaked in February 2022, with 100,000 or more cases. Subsequently, July 2022, the time of starting to write this chapter, saw the next outbreak.

To summarize, Japan has experienced several outbreaks of the virus, with the scale of the infection growing larger each time. In contrast, the number of deaths per day peaked at about 100 during 2020, which is very low given the size of Japan's total population. Most of the deaths were of the elderly; 94% of deaths occurred in people over the age of 60, and the percentage including those in their 50 s is 98%.

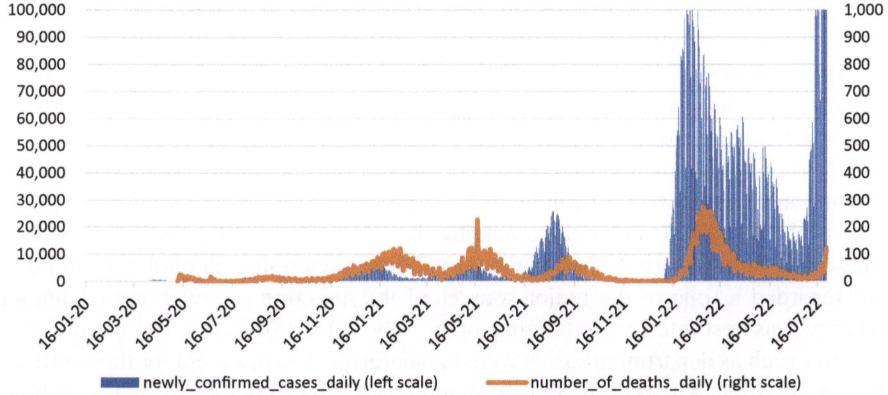

Fig. 1.1 The number of new COVID-19 infections and deaths in Japan. *Source* Created from materials from the Ministry of Health, Labor and Welfare of Japan (https://covid19.mhlw.go.jp/extensions/public/index.html, Accessed on July 29, 2022)

In other words, young people and those with children had little risk of dying from the coronavirus infection. While the number of new infections was much higher in the later waves, the number of deaths was not. This can be attributed to the spread of vaccination, improvement in the treatment system in hospitals, Japanese immunity, and the weakening of the virus toxicity.

The extent of damage by COVID-19 in Japan is easy to understand when compared with major Western and Asian countries (Table 1.1). Given that each country's population size varies greatly, it is necessary to compare the number of infected people and the number of deaths per unit population when comparing the damage of each country. In examining Table 1.1, it should be noted that the definitions of the number of infected cases and the number of deaths due to the virus, released by WHO, differ from country to country. For example, countries that actively carried out PCR tests may have found more infected cases. Also, in Japan, if a person who died was found to be infected with COVID-19, the death was counted as due to the virus, even if it was not the direct cause of their death. This means that the number of deaths counted by Japan may be higher than the actual number of deaths due to the virus. The cumulative number of infected people per 100,000 people in Japan is 9,399, and the number of deaths is 25. This is only a fraction of the number of infected cases in Western Europe and North America, while Japan's death toll is less than a tenth of theirs. Western Pacific countries generally have significantly lower rates of infections and deaths than Western European countries. Even compared to them, the number of infected cases and deaths per unit population remains low for Japan. It can hence be concluded that while Japan experienced multiple waves of COVID-19, it suffered relatively few *human damages* from the virus.

Responding to the virus outbreak, the Japanese government implemented various measures to prevent its spread. Of these, we will focus on the country's three emergency declarations, briefly describing their outline and characteristics (Table 1.2). While not mentioned here, Japan imposed weaker measures to prevent infection in the period between each declaration, which restricting the activities of individuals and companies based on *requests* from the central and local governments. It will be explained later that the *state of emergency* in Japan, unlike in major European countries, did not involve lockdowns of cities or legally enforceable restrictions on individual movements; it was a rather *loose* emergency declaration.

Japan's first state of emergency was declared in April and May 2020 as a countermeasure in seven prefectures, including Tokyo, where the infection spread rapidly. Among the three states of emergency, the first one imposed the strongest restrictions on economic activity and personal conduct. Given that alcohol consumption was regarded as one of the major sources of the infection's spread, the restaurant industry was restricted to remaining open only until 8:00 p.m., and commercial facilities such as department stores were mandatorily closed, except for those selling daily necessities. All sporting and entertainment events were canceled. Throughout Japan, elementary schools to universities had stopped in-person lessons for nearly the entire semester (Japanese schools start in April, with the first semester running from April to July). First implemented in Japan, this measure of closing schools for a certain period was followed by other Western countries, which henceforth normalized

Table 1.1 Number of COVID-19 infections and deaths in selected regions and countries

Name	Region	Cases—cumulative total	Cases—cumulative total per 100,000 population	Deaths—cumulative total	Deaths—cumulative total per 100,000 population
Republic of Korea	Western Pacific	1,95,35,242	38,103	24,957	49
Australia	Western Pacific	92,35,014	36,216	11,387	45
New Zealand	Western Pacific	15,85,215	32,873	2,117	44
Singapore	Western Pacific	16,85,889	28,817	1,490	25
Viet Nam	Western Pacific	1,07,72,980	11,068	43,092	44
Japan	Western Pacific	1,18,88,057	9,399	32,170	25
China	Western Pacific	55,41,446	377	23,434	2
Thailand	South-East Asia	45,84,070	6,567	31,290	45
India	South-East Asia	4,39,59,321	3,185	5,26,212	38
Indonesia	South-East Asia	61,91,664	2,264	1,56,957	57
United States of America	Americas	8,96,55,437	27,086	10,18,073	308
Canada	Americas	40,23,104	10,659	42,447	112
Denmark	Europe	32,26,717	55,416	6,623	114
France	Europe	3,27,23,365	50,313	1,48,357	228
Netherlands	Europe	83,24,399	47,821	22,483	129
Germany	Europe	3,07,02,511	36,917	1,43,702	173
Italy	Europe	2,08,37,233	34,937	1,71,439	287
The United Kingdom	Europe	2,33,04,931	34,330	1,83,953	271
Spain	Europe	1,32,03,228	27,895	1,10,394	233
Norway	Europe	14,54,928	27,106	3,623	67
Sweden	Europe	25,39,715	24,592	19,358	187

(continued)

Table 1.1 (continued)

Name	Region	Cases—cumulative total	Cases—cumulative total per 100,000 population	Deaths—cumulative total	Deaths—cumulative total per 100,000 population
Finland	Europe	11,71,032	21,194	5,012	91
Global		57,11,98,904	7,328	63,87,863	82

Source WHO Coronavirus (COVID-19) Dashboard (https://covid19.who.int/data, Accessed on July 29, 2022)

Table 1.2 Overview of Japan's declared state of emergency

	1st time	2nd time	3rd time
Period	April 7–May 25, 2020	January 8–March 21, 2021	April 25–September 30, 2021
Area	7 prefectures including Tokyo	4 prefectures in the Tokyo metropolitan area (7 prefectures added midway)	4 prefectures: Tokyo, Osaka, Kyoto, Hyogo (6 prefectures added midway)
Restaurant business	Until 8 pm	Until 8 pm	Until 8 pm, stores offering sake or karaoke are closed
Commercial facility	Closed (excluding daily necessities)	Until 8 pm	Closed (excluding daily necessities)
Event	Canceled or postponed	Up to 5,000 people and capacity rate within 50%	No audience in principle
School	Close school	Not close school	Not close school
Railway	No request to reduce trains	No request to reduce trains	Moving up the last train time on weekdays. Request to reduce trains on weekends and holidays
Remarks			Tokyo olympics: July 23–August 8, Tokyo Paralympics: August 24–September 5

Notes Created from government materials and the Yomiuri Shimbun article dated April 23, 2021

conducting online school classes. Even prior to the pandemic, the Japanese government had decided to distribute free tablet personal computers (PCs) to all elementary and junior high school students from the 2020 fiscal year, as part of *the GIGA School Concept*. Every school used this fortuitous event to conduct online classes for the first time, while universities urgently constructed environments of information technology (IT) to enable online classes, particularly in the Tokyo metropolitan area. In the meantime, the central and local governments requested companies to promote telework and reduce the number of employees physically present at their offices. While this was not legally binding, many Japanese companies responded positively, and the number of employees commuting to work decreased significantly. Of course, this also depended on the type of industry; telework was not possible for all occupations. Areas where no state of emergency was declared took roughly the same measures as those subject to the declaration.

The second state of emergency declaration, issued from January to March 2021 for large cities like the Tokyo metropolitan area, was more relaxed than the first one. In particular, restrictions on restaurant business hours were equally as strong as in the past, but commercial facilities remained operative. Schools were not ordered to close, and continued to hold regular classes while taking measures to prevent infection. Events were limited to 5,000 people and 50% capacity. Companies were still requested to promote telework.

The third declaration was issued from April to September 2021 for the four prefectures of Tokyo, Osaka, Kyoto, and Hyogo, with six additional prefectures added later. This was presumably aimed at suppressing COVID-19 in time for the Tokyo Olympics. The degree of infection control at this time was stronger than that of the second emergency. Restaurants could only be open until 8:00 p.m., whereas liquor and karaoke establishments were completely closed. Commercial facilities were also closed, except for daily necessities. Sports and other events, including the Tokyo Olympics games, in principle, were held without spectators; people watched the games on TV and the internet. Additionally, the railways in the declared areas were requested to schedule the last train on weekdays at an earlier time, and reduce the number of trains on weekends and holidays.

In summary, Japan's countermeasures against the pandemic have been more limited and relaxed than those in major European countries, where strong measures such as city-wide lockdowns were imposed. However, perhaps due to Japan's national character, the actual actions taken by citizens were quite strict. For example, even outside the state of emergency, everyone wore masks while stepping out or at work; this phenomenon was also remarked upon by the Western media. Telework was implemented in many companies, especially large ones, thus reducing the number of people commuting to work. Even after students returned to school for offline classes, transparent shields were set up on all desks to prevent students from talking to each other, and even school lunch was a *silent meal*. Restaurants remained deserted and travel across prefectural borders was greatly curtailed, thus deserting rural towns built on tourism. In other words, although Japan's countermeasures were superficially lax, people and companies conscientiously curbed their behavior and activities beyond the rules.

1.3 Impact of COVID-19 on Japan's Economic Activities

While Japan's countermeasures against COVID-19 have been generally milder than those of Western countries, its impact on Japanese society has not been insignificant. This is evident from statistics on Japan's macroeconomy. The Annual Report on the Japanese Economy and Public Finance 2020 (Cabinet Secretariat, 2020) prepared by the Japanese government describes the turmoil and stagnation of domestic economic activity in the year when the virus spread. Firstly, inbound demand disappeared; in pre-corona times, domestic tourism was doing well and there were a large number of foreigners visiting Japan. Subsequently, the supply chain was restricted due to the stagnation of production activities in China because of the spread of the infection, following which production activities in Japan were also delayed. Due to the countermeasures against the infection, Japanese domestic economic and social activities were forcibly restrained. Second, the suspension of economic activities by major trading partners had a tremendous impact on the Japanese economy, including a sharp decline in exports from Japan.

The magnitude of the impact on Japan's economic activity can be understood from changes in the country's economic growth rate during the pandemic. Figure 1.2 shows the quarter-on-quarter comparison of real gross domestic product between the period of the Lehman Shock, which occurred some 10 years ago, and the period of the current COVID-19 shock. The Lehman Brothers bankruptcy of September 2008 caused a major economic recession in developed countries. As can be seen from Fig. 1.2, the extent of the recession at this time was greater in Japan than in the United States (US), the United Kingdom (UK), and other countries. In contrast, fluctuations in the economic growth rate of each country during the current shock were much larger. For example, the rate in the first quarter (Q1) of 2020 was −19.4% in the UK, −13.7% in France, −8.9% in the US, and −7.9% in Japan. However, in the second half of 2020, Japan's economic growth recovery was weaker than that of the Western countries. After 2021, Japan's economic growth rate has been much slower than that of other countries.

The fluctuation in Japan's economic growth rate reflects the characteristics of its countermeasures against COVID-19. As described above, the number of people infected with the virus in Japan was smaller than in major Western countries, hence the country's infection control measures were lax. Accordingly, during the onset of the pandemic in the first half of 2020, Japan's rate of economic deceleration was milder than in other countries, although the rate of decline was much larger than that during the Lehman Shock. However, Japan's countermeasures have been sluggish and long-term, and the Japanese people have continued to *rigidly* take infection control measures and restrain their behavior; as a result, the troughs of Japanese

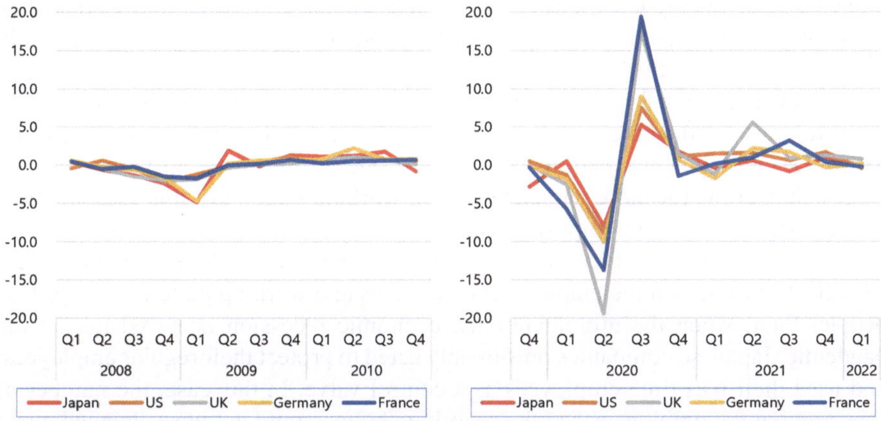

Fig. 1.2 Quarterly change in real gross domestic product: comparison between the Lehman shock and the COVID-19 shock (unit: %). *Notes* Real gross domestic product is adjusted quarterly and seasonally. *Source* Created from materials released by the Japan Institute for Labor Policy and Training (https://www.jil.go.jp/kokunai/statistics/covid-19/f/f61.html, accessed on July 31, 2022)

economic activity were not deep, but the peaks that followed were small, and the economy continued to fly low.

1.4 Impact of COVID-19 on Japanese Work and Family Life

The COVID-19 crisis has also had a macro impact on microaspects of Japanese society, such as the attitude and behavior of individuals. This book focuses on three such uniquely characterized areas: employment and telework, family life, and family formation under low fertility. These Japanese characteristics are briefly described in this section, together with the pandemic's impact on them. Each characteristic is detailed in its own chapter.

1.4.1 Employment and Telework

Japanese employment and work pattern characteristics are shaped by *Japanese-style employment practices*, which include the collective hiring of new graduates, seniority-based wage system, lifetime employment, and membership-type employment contracts with unlimited job extension (Matsuda & Sasaki, 2020; Matsuda, 2021). However, new graduates with regular employment receive higher wages than others under the seniority-based system. Firms rarely fire regular employees unless facing a financial crisis, and these employees work diligently and devote themselves to the company, being known as *company men/ women* and *workaholics*, since they work long hours. In addition, the average Japanese commute is very long, especially in the big cities, lengthening the daily sum of working hours for regular employees, and making it difficult for them to balance work and family life, especially for women with children. On the other hand, it is not easy for part-time employees to transition to regular employment positions. While part-time positions are unstable with low wages, they allow for more choice regarding working hours. For that reason, many women with children are employed as non-regular workers in Japan.

Specifically, we will focus on the following two points addressing the impact COVID-19 has had on the employment situations and working patterns of Japanese people. First, when the aforementioned economic recession occurred due to the pandemic, Japanese companies presumably acted to protect their regular employees, and used their part-time employees as a control valve. In this case, the number of Japanese regular employees and their working hours would not have changed much during the pandemic, while the number and working hours of part-time employees would have decreased significantly.

Second, while telework was primarily promoted to prevent the spread of corona, it also worked to release Japanese workers from the challenges of long working hours and commutes, improving their work-life balance. Since telework enables both men and women with children to work at home, it may have adjusted the disproportionate distribution of housework burdens on wives. However, since the rate of telework varies depending on the type of industry and job, not all Japanese workers can reap the benefit.

1.4.2 Family Life

The traditional gender division of labor remains strong in Japan. Although women's social advancement has seen considerable progress, it is the husband who takes on the main earning role, while the wife mainly takes care of housework and child-rearing for many couples. The average amount of time spent daily on housework in 2016 was 49 min for husbands, and 4 h and 55 min for wives (Statistics Bureau of Japan, 2017), indicating the significant difference between genders. In addition to the influence of traditional gender norms, another reason for this difference is the difference in husbands' and wives' work style. In many families, husbands work long into the night as regular employees, while the wives work part-time or stay at home. Moreover, the use of domestic servants by the middle or upper class is not a cultural norm in Japan, unlike other developed countries, requiring Japanese wives to spend considerable time doing housework themselves. This disproportionate share of the domestic work increases the burden on the wife, and has been argued to be one of the reasons for Japan's low fertility rates (Tsuya et al., 2019).

COVID-19 may have had an impact on these family roles. In fact, there were factors that could both weaken and strengthen the wife's bias in the role of housework during the pandemic. The promotion of telework is thought to have contributed to weakening the traditional gender division of labor within couples, weakening the bias toward the wife's side. As mentioned above, not only do the Japanese work longer hours, but they also face longer commutes, especially for those in the Tokyo metropolitan area. Eliminating commuting times, telework allows these workers to save more than two hours a day. Given that the most apparent determinant of Japanese men's participation in housework and childcare is the length of their working hours (Matsuda, 2021), teleworking men could use that time for household chores and childcare.

On the other hand, school closures and online classes may have contributed to strengthen the gender division of labor, that is, the bias toward the wife's side. In addition, many women who work while raising children are part-time employees. Due to the economic recession, the number of part-time employees has decreased, and their working hours have been reduced. These changes suggest that wives may have been more likely to stay at home and take care of household chores and childcare.

1.4.3 Family Formation Under Low Fertility

Prior to the pandemic, Japan had experienced a long-term stagnation of its birth rate, becoming a *shrinking society* (Hara, 2015). Japan's total fertility rate in 2019 was 1.36. The 2019 fertility rates in Western countries were 1.65 for the UK, 1.84 for France, 1.54 for Germany, 1.27 for Italy, 1.70 for Sweden, and 1.71 for the US. Cohabitation and children born out of wedlock are not socially prevalent in Japan; the country's declining birthrate is thus related to a decline in marriage. The gradual decline in the number of children that couples have has further contributed to the sluggish fertility in recent years (Matsuda, 2021; Suzuki, 2013). Overall, Japan's declining birthrate has been caused by several major factors, including the deterioration of youth employment, the increasing burden of educational expenses on families, and the difficulty of balancing work and child-rearing for women (Matsuda & Sasaki, 2020; Matsuda, 2021).

While Japan was the first East Asian country to experience a declining birth rate, countries/regions like South Korea, China, and Taiwan have also recently suffered from greater birth rate declines than Japan. Japan is a unique country that has sustained its birth rate at a certain level compared to other East Asian countries, even though it is suffering from low fertility. This is because Japanese women's childbirth, educational background, and employment patterns are more diversified compared to other East Asian countries, and first, second, and third child birth rates among married Japanese women have not declined as much as in China and South Korea (Tsuya et al., 2019).

Birth rates have fallen in many developed countries during the current pandemic, including Japan. Specifically, COVID-19 may have had the following effects on marriage and childbirth in Japan. There have been various news reports of young Japanese couples postponing their weddings during the pandemic. Similarly, it is possible that many couples postponed having children during the pandemic, due to fear of infection, or due to unstable employment and income. Furthermore, telework and moving restrictions exacerbated the lack of opportunities to meet a romantic partner.

The changes described above are our theoretical assumptions. To our knowledge, few research has yet been published in Japan on these factors. Through empirical evidence, this book reveals how the pandemic has impacted people's work and family life in Japan, which has a different social background from Western countries.

References

Cabinet Secretariat. (2020). *The annual report on the Japanese economy and public finance 2020*. https://www5.cao.go.jp/keizai3/2020/1106wp-keizai/setsumei-e2020.pdf. Accessed 30 July 2022.

Hara, T. (2015). *A shrinking society: Post-demographic transition in Japan*. Springer.

Matsuda, S., & Sasaki, T. (2020). Deteriorating employment and marriage decline in Japan. *Comparative Population Studies, 45*, 395–416.

Matsuda, S. (2021). *[Sequel] The theory of declining birth rate: Recovery of birth rate and society with free choices*. Gakubunsha [in Japanese].

National Institute of Infectious Diseases. (2020). *IDWR No. 21 of 2020 infectious diseases to watch novel coronavirus infection (COVID-19)*. https://www.niid.go.jp/niid/ja/2019-ncov/2487-idsc/idwr-topic/9669-idwrc-2021.html. Accessed 30 July 2022.

Statistics Bureau of Japan. (2017). Summary of results of 2016 survey on time use and leisure activities. http://www.stat.go.jp/english/data/shakai/2016/pdf/timeuse-a2016.pdf. Accessed 30 July 2022.

Suzuki, T. (2013). *Low fertility and population aging in Japan and Eastern Asia*. Springer.

Tsuya, O. N., Minja, K. C., & Feng, W. (2019). *Convergence to very low fertility in East Asia: Processes, causes, and implications*. Springer.

World Health Organization. (2020). *WHO coronavirus (COVID-19), dashboard*. https://covid19.who.int/data. Accessed 31 July 2022.

Chapter 2
How Does Telework Contribute to Generating Inequality During the COVID-19 Pandemic? The New Origin of Inequality in Japan

JaeYoul Shin and Hirohisa Takenoshita

Abstract In this chapter, we examine the inequality structure in telework engagement and the impact of telework on working conditions using policy materials issued by the Japanese government and major research institutes and the Survey on Work and Life under COVID-19 (WLCV survey). According to findings, the COVID-19 pandemic is the most important momentum about telework diffusion in Japan. Interestingly, in Japan, the dual structure of the labor market has been reproduced in telework implementation and teleworkers' working conditions. Highly-skilled or educated workers can easily work at home. Regular workers or workers in large firms participate in telework more than non-regular workers or workers in small and medium-sized firms. In addition, telework affects working conditions, but the direction is different by gender. While telework improves job satisfaction among male workers, it reduces satisfaction among female workers. Those findings indicate that the gender inequality in family responsibility that existed in Japanese society is reflected in telework practice as it is. To summarize, telework implementation could deteriorate inequality in the labor market. Therefore, researchers need to consider how telework can be used as a tool for the reduction of inequality and improvement in working conditions.

Keywords telework · Work from home · SBTC hypothesis · COVID-19 · Telework implementation · Job satisfaction

J. Shin (✉)
Hiroshima University, Higashi-Hiroshima, Japan
e-mail: rec419@hanmail.net

H. Takenoshita
Keio University, Tokyo, Japan

S. Matsuda and H. Takenoshita (eds.), *Changes in Work and Family Life in Japan Under COVID-19*, Population Studies of Japan, https://doi.org/10.1007/978-981-99-5850-4_2

2.1 Introduction

The first academic research on telework was in the field of transportation (Pérez et al., 2004a, 2004b). Telework generally refers to the working practices in which people do their job away from the office by using information and communication technology (ICT) (Hill et al., 2003). In early studies, scholars expected telework to function as a tool that would effectively help solve social problems, such as traffic jams, natural disasters, regional inequalities, pollution, and energy inefficiency (Di Martino & Wirth, 1990; Grimes, 1992; Nilles, 1975; Rietveld, 2011). In this context, some countries tried to implement policies for the spread of telework; the Nordic telecottages in the 1980s are a well-known example (Qvortrup, 1989).[1] There was a movement to popularize telework in Japan as well. In the 1990s, in particular, research on telework was active, and even now, telework policies are being implemented.[2] However, the spread of telework is still delayed, not only in Japan but also in other countries (Hynes, 2016).

In addition, some research is concerned about how telework helps workers balance work and family life. The issue of work-family balance is highly critical to married women with children, given the gender inequality in family responsibilities. Telework allows workers to engage in their job outside their offices and to avoid commuting travel between home and workplace, thereby increasing work flexibility in location and time (Maruyama et al., 2009). Thus, it is sociologically relevant to investigate the inequality in access to telework among workers who have young children.

The environment surrounding the diffusion of telework changed dramatically due to the COVID-19 (SARS-CoV-2 virus) pandemic, which required organizations to introduce telework into workplaces to prevent workers' exposure to infectious disease. According to the JILPT (The Japan Institute for Labour Policy and Training, 2021), before COVID-19 in 2019, only 25.6% of workers had engaged in telework, but in March 2021, 57.6% of workers were teleworking. This means that many organizations introduced telework in response to the COVID-19 pandemic. By participating in telework, workers could protect themselves against the risk of infection while securing their employment and earning as much as they had before the pandemic.

Nevertheless, not all workers could participate in telework. The participation rate differs by occupation. While sales workers and manufacturing workers are usually required to go into their workplaces, workers who have high ICT skills are able to switch to telework more easily than other workers. For many years, inequality

[1] The Nordic countries—Denmark, Norway, Sweden, and Finland—established the first telecottages in September 1988. The telecottages are officially named community teleservice centers. Qvortrup defines the telecottage as 'a centre where IT apparatus is placed at the disposal of the citizens of a specific local community within a marginal geographical location, so that communal use may be made of the facilities available' (Qvortrup, 1989).

[2] The Japan Telework Association or Tokyo Foundation for Employment Services are representative examples. The Ministry of Health, Labor and Welfare and the Japan Telework Association award a ministerial commendation called 'Kagayaku Telework' each year. For more specific information, please refer to kagayakutelework.jp, telework.mhlw.go.jp, or japan-telework.or.jp.

researchers have been concerned about the role of technology in changing inequality and how people work (Erikson & Goldthorpe, 1992). As telework requires people to use ICT skills, it is reasonable to claim that access to telework depends on workers' ICT skills. Inequality in access to telework would also lead to inequality in life chances in other domains: employment, income, and health. Hence, participation in telework is an important research topic for understanding the social inequality that has arisen in the pandemic era.

Given its sociological importance, this study explores how telework creates inequality in the labor market. This study explores the inequality structure that originated from access to telework and how telework creates social inequalities in the COVID-19 pandemic era. This study focuses on married couples with children because these individuals need to cope with balancing work and family life and because the closure of school and childcare facilities in 2020 hindered parents from working away from home. Above all, this study investigates how inequality in access to telework differs between men and women because the availability of telework is highly crucial to married women, who have greater family responsibility than men. To explore this issue, we rely on theories of stratification and inequality. As argued above, we pay attention to the role of ICT skills in shaping inequality in access to telework. The human capital perspective provides researchers with some clues for investigating inequality in telework. Theories of the segmented labor market also help us consider how the Japanese inequality structure is reflected in and reinforced by access to home-based telework.

The structure of this article is as follows. First, we present the scope and definition of telework. Second, we review the previous research on who can choose to telework, how ICT and the COVID-19 pandemic affect access to telework, and the consequences of telework. Third, we elaborate on the history of telework in Japan. Fourth, we explain analytical strategies. Fifth, we describe our data and methods. Sixth, we show our results regarding access to telework and its determinants and consequences. In this section, we explain how telework makes and reproduces social inequality. Finally, we summarize our results and discuss the implications of our study.

2.2 Previous Research

2.2.1 Scope and Definition of Telework

Generally, telework can be understood as an alternative work arrangement based on ICT (Frolick et al., 1993; Pérez et al., 2002). Nilles (1975) argues that ICT is a key determinant of telework. The effects of ICT on the introduction of telework are evident (Di Martino & Wirth, 1990; Gareis et al., 2004; Pérez et al., 2004a, 2004b; Popuri & Bhat, 2001; Stanworth, 1998; Wellman et al., 1996). Recently, the International Labor Organization (ILO) suggested that telework refers to the use of ICT provided by the employer to complete work outside the office (ILO, 2020; Ravalet & Rérat, 2019). In Japan, the Tokyo Metropolitan Government (TMG) defined telework in the '2022 Report on the results of the survey on diverse work style (telework)' as 'A flexible working style that utilizes ICT, such as personal computers, smartphones, and tablet terminals, to make effective usage of time and place.' Therefore, the use of ICT provided by the employer is important for completing work outside the office (Belzunegui-Eraso & Erro-Garcés, 2020; Kelly, 1988; Mokhtarian, 1991).

However, there is no consensus regarding the definition of telework; rather, slightly different definitions and scopes have been proposed. Di Martino and Wirth (1990) mention that the definition of telework needs to cover a variety of situations. Sullivan (2003) defines telework as remote work using ICT, but it can also be defined in consideration of transportation, work location, the percentage of time spent working, and contractual arrangements. Generally, telework can be roughly categorized into three categories: home office, mobile office, and virtual office (Gareis et al., 2004; Hill et al. 2003; Messenger & Gschwind, 2016; TMG, 2022).[3] However, most scholars who study telework generally tend to focus on home offices based on ICT. In Japan, according to the '2022 Report on the results of the survey on diverse work style (telework),' while 98.2% of 1449 companies perform home-based telework, 23.1% implement mobile telework, 6.1% of companies operate satellite offices (TMG 2022). In this context, we define telework as working at home with ICT.

2.2.2 *Utilization of ICT, SBTC Hypothesis, and Telework Practice*

As mentioned above, working on the job which require utilizing ICT skills and having educational attainment for learning of ICT skills are important factors of telework practice (Messenger & Gschwind, 2016; Thulin et al., 2019; Vilhelmson & Thulin, 2016). To understand and explain the role of ICT in telework practice, this study applies the skill-biased technological change (SBTC) hypothesis to understand telework practices and the implementation and consequences of telework. Originally, the SBTC hypothesis was established to explain the rising wage inequality in the US after the 1980s. It argues that the development of computer technology caused a rise in the demand for highly skilled workers who can use ICT tools and computers for their job, while computerization and digitalization in workplaces led to the declining demand for workers to carry out a set of routine manual and cognitive tasks (Autor et al., 2003; Card & DiNardo, 2002). Hence, such changes in skill demand contributed to the widening wage gap between highly skilled and unskilled workers.

Therefore, how workers can use ICT in their jobs shapes whether they can do their tasks remotely (Bélanger, 1999; Boell et al., 2016; Di Martino & Wirth, 1990). Given the differences in the availability of ICT by occupation, inequality in the telework participation rate across occupations is inevitable. If workers are in white-collar

[3] Messenger and Gschwind (2016) propose the expression 'three generations'.

or knowledge-oriented sectors, they are more likely to implement telework (Mayo et al., 2016). For example, in the US, telework is most widely available for computer and mathematical occupations; education, training, and library occupations; legal occupations; business and financial operations occupations; and management occupations. Currently, 37% of workers can perform their jobs through telework without commuting (Dingel & Neiman, 2020). In Japan, ICT skills are also closely related to telework practice. Okubo (2022) shows that ICT skills positively affect workers' participation in telework; however, if a worker's task is routinized, it is difficult to participate in telework. Ishii et al. (2021) and Kawaguchi and Motegi (2021) find similar findings. For similar reasons, the possibility of teleworking varies by industry. In the US, more than 80% of people were found able to work at home in the professional, scientific, and technical services sector; the management of companies and enterprises sector; the educational services sector; the finance and insurance sector; and the information sector (Dingel & Neiman, 2020).

Educational attainment is closely related to telework practice in the context of the STBC hypothesis. Generally, learning and utilizing ICT skills require more knowledge-intensive activities, and it is easy for highly educated workers to meet these requirements. Reasonably, highly educated workers are more likely to engage in telework than lower-educated workers, and vocational field and qualification level are other important factors that determine telework status (Di Martino & Wirth, 1990; Dingel & Neiman, 2020; Haddon & Brynin, 2005; Hjorthol, 2006; Natti et al., 2011; Walls et al., 2010). Consequently, education is directly related to inequality in access to telework (Peters et al., 2004).

Finally, we also need to consider that establishing a telework system requires ICT-intensive human power and capital. In other words, it is difficult to introduce telework into small and medium-sized enterprises (SMEs) for technical and organizational reasons (Gareis et al., 2004; Grimes, 1992). According to Ishii et al. (2021), the company's scale and management ability are quite important factors in implementing telework in Japan. In their analysis, the possibility of telework is proportional to the company scale: the possibility of telework is approximately 0.1 for companies with fewer than 30 persons but approximately 0.3 for those with 300–1000 persons and 0.4 for those with over 1000 persons. Similarly, Okubo (2022) argues that not only individual factors but also the working environment and digitalization are important factors in Japan. In his analysis, 78% of teleworkers utilize ICT tools, but only 21% of nonteleworkers use ICT tools in their office. The digitalization and automation of offices improve the possibility of telework.[4]

[4] They do not directly mention the SBTC hypothesis, but their argument and analysis support the SBTC hypothesis.

2.2.3 COVID-19 Pandemic as an Environmental Factor

As mentioned above, technological development is a critical determinant of telework (Gilbert, 1996); however, ICT is not a sufficient condition for its introduction (Elldér, 2019; Haddon & Brynin, 2005; Hjorthol, 2006; Scott et al., 2012). ICT is only a prerequisite for the spread of telework (Haddon & Brynin, 2005). Rather, ICT depends on social relationships (Howcroft & Rubery, 2019). The introduction of telework is determined by technological factors, organizational factors, home-family factors, environmental factors, and legal factors (Belzunegui-Eraso & Erro-Garcés, 2020). Some scholars have argued that ICT has nothing to do with teleworking (Bélanger, 1999; Elldér, 2019; Pérez et al., 2004a, 2004b). Thus, the claim that telework is possible only for ICT-related workers is inaccurate (Stanworth, 1998).

Frankly, the effects of environmental changes are the most critical and important determinants of telework (Baruch & Nicholson, 1997). It should not be overlooked that at the outset, telework emerged from the oil crisis of the 1970s, which is why the first study of telework was in the field of transportation (Bailey & Kurland, 2002; Pérez et al., 2004a, 2004b). Moreover, due to its freedom from spatial constraints, telework was gradually examined as a method for executing business during disasters. For example, telework was used substantially in New Zealand from September 2010 to January 2012 because of consecutive earthquakes in Christchurch (Donnelly & Proctor-Thomson, 2015).

The recent rapid spread of telework was triggered by the COVID-19 pandemic. The COVID-19 pandemic has forced firms to implement telework to a greater degree than traditional disaster situations. Many studies have shown that COVID-19 has stimulated telework (Belzunegui-Eraso & Erro-Garcés, 2020; Diab-Bahman & Al-Enzi, 2020; Dingel & Neiman, 2020; Tavares et al., 2020). For example, according to Eurofound (2020), the %age of telework that started because of COVID-19 is quite high, reaching, for example, almost 60% in Finland. It is appropriate to explain this increase in telework as resulting from COVID-19 rather than technological development in 2020 (Agba et al., 2020; ILO, 2020; OECD, 2020). In the United States, in February 2020, only 8.2% of workers participated in home-based telework, but in May 2020, 35.2% of workers became teleworkers (Bick et al., 2020). Brynjolfsson et al. (2020) find that a doubling in COVID-19 infection leads to an approximately 5% increase in telework. Japan is no exception. Kawashima et al. (2021) show that increasing the fever rate leads to more implementation of telework. Okubo (2022) finds that the spread of COVID-19 accompanies the extension of telework. Additionally, much survey research shows a rapid increase in telework in Japan. Interestingly, with the stablilization of the COVID-19 pandemic, many companies have quit implementing telework and returned to the traditional working style. For example, the large IT companies Apple, Google, and Meta in the US; Kakao, Nexon, and Naver in Korea; and Honda and Rakuten in Japan terminated or drastically reduced the implementation of telework.[5] We explore this in more detail with a focus on Japan's case in the next section.

2.2.4 The Consequences of Telework

Nilles (1976a, 1976b) already discussed the condition for implementing telework, the various effects of telework on workers, and the attitude toward telework of employees and employers. Simply put, his early studies touched all issues related to telework. Studies on telework stagnated after Nilles (1975). After Nilles (1975), researchers began to consider the consequences of telework. Scholars mainly examined how telework contributes to work-life balance, working conditions, and job performance. In this section, we examine work-life balance and working conditions.

First, regarding job satisfaction, the results are inconsistent. Bailey and Kurland (2002) mentioned that there are no consistent results on the effects of telework on job satisfaction. Nevertheless, some studies report the positive effects of telework on working conditions, such as job satisfaction and working hours. Shin (2021) examined the case of Korea in 2021 and observed a positive effect of telework on wages, job satisfaction, life satisfaction, and happiness. He used a Korean labor and income panel study to check how telework affects working conditions in the context of the COVID-19 pandemic. He found a clear relationship between doing telework and increasing wages. Additionally, workers who implement telework report higher job satisfaction, life satisfaction, and happiness. In Japan, Minetake (2020) reports the positive effect of telework on happiness.

Second, regarding work-life balance, some studies have reported that telework is useful only for men, not women. Most studies demonstrate that telework does not influence the division of household chores between husbands and wives during the COVID-19 pandemic. According to Del Boca et al. (2020), female workers who participate in telework report more hardship in work-life balance than male workers. Even though the husband engages in childcare and housekeeping, the contribution is limited. Eventually, wives take on most of the burden of housework when they and their partners engage in telework (Adams-Prassl et al., 2020; Del Boca et al., 2020; Hupkau & Petrongolo, 2020; Ohtani, 2021; Sakuragi et al., 2022; Sevilla & Smith, 2020; Son, 2022). Del Boca et al. (2020) show that for women, telework still creates difficulties in work-life balance, and the husband's telework does not improve women's work-life balance. Moreover, according to Son (2022), since the COVID-19 pandemic, women's housework and childcare time have significantly increased. The most serious point is that compared to nonteleworking women, women who engage in telework confront increasing time spent on housework and childcare after COVID-19. We can also find the same tendency in Japan. Sakuragi et al. (2022) report how COVID-19 has changed the burden of housework and childcare. Their research shows

[5] For example: https://www.forbes.com/sites/glebtsipursky/2022/11/22/google-and-apples-myth-of-losing-social-capital-in-hybrid-work/?sh=35b9a2cc5584.

the negative effect of telework on time spent on housework and childcare, with a stronger negative effect on women. A total of 34.3% of male workers who implement telework more than 2 days a week report increased time spent on housework and childcare, but 52.7% of female workers report increased time. Interestingly, Hupkau and Petrongolo (2020) report similar results. In the UK from 2014 to 2020, fathers' childcare time increased from under 8 h to 14.8 h (an increase of 6.9 extra hours), but mothers' childcare time increased from 17 to 26.5 h (an increase of 9.5 extra hours). Additionally, Ohtani (2021) argues that the implementation of telework forced women to do work and housework at the same time. From those contexts, we may easily assume that achieving work-life balance by implementing telework is possible only for men, not women.

2.2.5 *Context of Telework in Japan*

2.2.5.1 Telework Before COVID-19

Telework was introduced relatively early in Japan, beginning in 1984. As part of the Nippon Telegraph and Telephone Corporation's (NTT's)[6] large-scale social experiment (INS experiment),[7] Nippon Electronic Company, Limited (NEC) set up a satellite office in Kichijoji, Musashino, Tokyo, which is geographically more convenient than its headquarters in Minato Ward, Tokyo, to promote the participation and employment retention of married women with infants in the labor market. In general, scholars and the government have shown that this social experiment was the first telework attempt in Japan. In this experiment, NEC provided personal computers to employees working at satellite offices for more effective task performance.

However, telework was practically introduced in Japan after the late 1980s. From 1986 to 1991, Japan went through an economic bubble. At that time, the concentration in the Tokyo metropolitan area became more serious. As a result, rents in the 23 wards of Tokyo were extremely high, so many office workers spent long hours commuting from the outer suburbs of Tokyo to downtown. According to the Ministry of Internal Affairs and Communications (MIC), during the period of the economic bubble, office maintenance costs per person in the 23 wards of Tokyo reached 3 million yen per year, and the average commuting time was approximately two hours. On the other hand, the NTT started the Integrated Service Digital Network (ISDN) in 1988, and a friendly technical environment for telework was established. As a result, some companies started to introduce satellite offices in consideration of the high rents in central Tokyo and the long commuting distance between the head office and residential areas of workers. Against this background, in 1988, companies such as Kajima Corporation, Uchida Yoko, and Mitsubishi Materials Corporation established

[6] For more specific information about NTT, please refer to this website: https://group.ntt/en/group/history/.

[7] For more details about the INS experiment, please refer to Takahashi (1986).

satellite offices in Saitama Prefecture near Tokyo. In particular, in 1991, the NTT established massive satellite offices in Saitama Prefecture, Kanagawa Prefecture, and Chiba Prefecture. Telework was introduced in Japan for the purpose of dispersing the population and preventing traffic jams (MIC 2010). At that time, the Japan Satellite Office Association (the name of the association was changed to the Japan Telework Association in 2000) was established in January 1991 as the first nongovernmental organization[8] that aimed to spread telework to private sectors. However, in 1992, the economic bubble burst, most satellite offices were closed, and the spread of telework slowed (MIC 2010).

After that, in 1996, the Ministry of Health, Labor and Welfare (MHLW) and the MIC promoted the Telework Project as part of 'the local area living information infrastructure enhancement project'[9] (MIC 1994). This project started to encourage the introduction of telework to private sectors. In the period of the economic bubble, some enterprises introduced telework to reduce the excessively high rent fees in central Tokyo and to some extent reduce workers' fatigue from long commuting times. Moreover, the Japanese government pushed to introduce and spread telework to promote the use of ICT as a new national growth strategy. In particular, after 2007, the Abe government promoted telework as part of long-term growth strategy guidelines called 'Innovation 25'[10] and presented the 'Telework population doubling action plan'[11] aimed at supporting work-life balance (Cabinet Office 2007). Additionally, in July 2009, the Abe government announced a plan to increase the number of teleworkers to 7 million by 2015 through the 'i-Japan Strategy 2015' and the 'New Information and Communications Technology Strategy' (IT Strategic Headquarters, 2010; MIC 2010).[12] More fundamentally, telework was implemented to achieve the neoliberal labor policies that accompany the demanded improvement in corporate efficiency. Recently, however, telework has been actively being used as a method for decentralization and regional revitalization centering on the Cabinet Secretariat. In the Cabinet Secretariat, the 'Recreation Headquarters Office of Town People Work and Life'[13] has been installed to encourage emigration to rural areas and disperse the population into various regions since 2017 (the first Cabinet decision was announced on December 27, 2016). The specific trends of law and policy related to telework are as follows.

In terms of policy for telework, the Cabinet Secretariat's 'Recreation Headquarters Office of Town People Work and Life' is representative. The most comprehensive collaboration and policy enforcement is taking place in this organization. Major government organizations, such as the Ministry of Foreign Affairs of Japan, the Ministry of Finance, Japan, and the Financial Services Agency as well as the Ministry of Health, Labor and Welfare (MHLW) participate in the secretariat. Here,

[8] For more specific information, please refer to this website: https://japan-telework.or.jp/outline/.

[9] In Japanese Chiiki seikatsu jōhōkihan kōdo-ka jigy.

[10] In Japanese Inobēshon 25.

[11] In Japanese Terewāku jinkō baizō akushon puran.

[12] https://warp.ndl.go.jp/info:ndljp/pid/12187388/japan.kantei.go.jp/policy/it/index_e.html.

[13] In Japanese, Machi hito shi-goto sōsei honbu jimukyoku.

the MHLW and Ministry of Land, Infrastructure, Transport, and Tourism (MLIT) are in charge of telework-related tasks. Of course, the MHLW, MIC, Ministry of Economy, Trade and Industry (METI), and MLIT have carried out various policies and investigative activities to promote telework. In 1999, the MIC entrusted the preparation of telework manuals (the 'Telework Tools List (7.0th Edition)[14]' is the current edition) to the Japan Telework Association, established in 1991. In this context, the 'communication usage trend survey (Businesses)'[15] began to ask about the current status of telework implementation in the 1999 survey by the MIC.[16] In February 2009, the four ministries jointly created and distributed 'The Telework GUIDEBOOK: Telework Introduction and Operation Guidebook for Enterprises'.[17] In addition, the MLIT conducted a 'Population Survey on Teleworkers' after 2002 to confirm the status of telework. The MIC has produced and distributed 'Telework Security Guidelines',[18] the 'Implementation guide for business owners',[19] and the 'Municipalities Telework Implementation Guide'[20] since 2006.

As a result of various policies, according to the '2021 Communication usage trend survey (Businesses)' conducted by the MIC, 0.8% of the companies surveyed in 1999 answered that they were implementing telework, but in 2019, 20.1% of companies answered that they were implementing telework (MIC 2022). Additionally, the '2008 Population Survey on Teleworkers' conducted by the MLIT reported that the telework rate increased from 6.1% in 2002 to 15.2% in 2008 and estimated that the rate would reach 20% in 2010 (MLIT 2009). In fact, the rate of telework increased until 2012: 16.5% in 2010, 19.7% in 2011, and 21.3% in 2012. However, after 2012, it presented a decreasing trend, reaching 17.3% in 2013 and 16.4% in 2014. The telework participation rate stagnated at 15.5% in 2017, 17.4% in 2018, and 15.4% in 2019 (MLIT 2014). On the other hand, according to the 'Survey on the state of telework in enterprises' conducted by the Japan Institute for labor policy and training (JILPT) in 2008, 5.3% of companies introduced full telework, 5.6% of companies introduced partial telework, 9.4% of companies introduced mobile work, and 7.3% of companies introduced satellite offices (JILPT 2008).[21] Consequently, despite various policy implementations, it is reasonable to assume that the penetration rate of telework was stagnant until 2019.

[14] In Japanese, Terewāku kanren tsūru ichiran (dai 7. 0 S-ban).

[15] https://www.soumu.go.jp/main_sosiki/joho_tsusin/eng/pressrelease/2020/5/29_6.html.

[16] https://www.soumu.go.jp/johotsusintokei/statistics/statistics05b2.html.

[17] https://www.mlit.go.jp/crd/daisei/telework/guidebook/guidebook.html.

[18] In Japanese, Terewākusekyuritigaidorain.

[19] In Japanese, Kigyō no keiei-sha-muke dōnyū gaido.

[20] In Japanese, Jichitai terewāku dōnyū gaido.

[21] https://www.jil.go.jp/institute/research/2008/050.html.

2.2.5.2 Telework After COVID-19

The dramatic spread of telework in Japan was triggered by the spread of COVID-19. First, according to the '2021 Population Survey on Teleworkers', the proportion of teleworkers stagnated until 2019, with rates of 14.2% in 2016, 15.5% in 2017, 17.4% in 2018, and 15.4% in 2019. However, with the outbreak of the COVID-19 pandemic, the rate of telework implantation doubled to 22.5% in 2020 and 27.1% in 2021. In addition, before February 2020, approximately 10.3% of companies used the telework system, but in April 2020, the figure nearly tripled to 29.3%. Of course, since then, the number of companies using telework has decreased somewhat, with 28.8% in July 2021 and 24.1% in October 2021, but it can be seen that more than twice as many companies are using telework compared to 2020 (MLIT 2022).[22] In the MIC's '2021 Communication usage trend survey (Businesses)', the telework introduction rate, which was 20.1% in 2018, increased significantly to 47.4% in 2020 and 51.8% in 2021 (MIC 2022). Additionally, according to the '2022 Report on the results of the survey on diverse work style (telework)' for companies with 30 or more employees in the Tokyo metropolitan area conducted by the Tokyo Metropolitan Government, the rate of telework was just 6.8% in 2017, 19.2% in 2018, and 25.1% in 2019, but after the COVID-19 pandemic, it reached 57.8% in July 2020, 58.8% in December 2020, and 65.7% in 2021 (TMG 2022).

In addition, several research institutes and research teams have conducted surveys to confirm the status of telework since COVID-19 began to spread in Japan in February 2020. A representative survey among them is the 'JILPT Panel Survey on the Impact of COVID-19 on Enterprise Management'. This survey is an internet panel survey of companies conducted six times, from the first survey in June 2020 to February 2022. According to the survey, only 5.0% of companies implemented telework in February 2020, but this Fig. 2.1 grew by nearly 5 times to 24.6% in March and rapidly increased by 12 times to 60.0% in April. Despite a decreasing trend of 58.8% in May, 47.9% in June, 42.9% in July, 40.0% in August, 39.6% in September, and 37.1% in October, 44.2% of companies still implemented telework as of January 2022 (JILPT 2022).[23]

Interestingly, most surveys report a gap in the telework participation rate according to region, occupation, industry, company size, and employment scale. First, what can be seen most clearly is the regional disparities. At the outset, the purpose of telework was to ease concentration and promote decentralization in large cities, but when the COVID-19 pandemic occurred, telework was most actively conducted in the metropolitan area. According to the '2021 Population Survey on Teleworkers', the average implementation rate of telework in 2019 was 18.8% in the Tokyo metropolitan area and 14.8% nationwide. However, after the COVID-19 pandemic in 2020, the national average increased 1.5 times to 23.0% in 2020 and 27.0% in 2021.

---

[22] Only for hired employees, excluding self-employed/freelancers.

[23] https://www.jil.go.jp/tokusyu/covid-19/press/index.html.

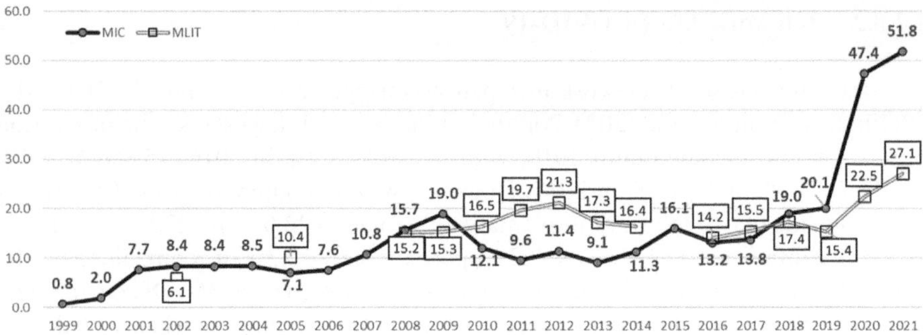

Fig. 2.1 Trends of telework in Japan from 1999. *Source* Communication usage trend survey (Businesses), MIC, 1999–2021
Population Survey on Teleworkers, MLIT, 2002–2021

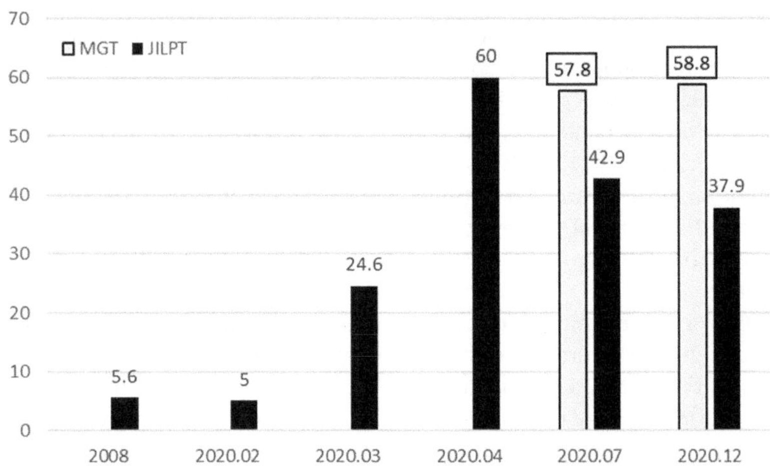

Fig. 2.2 Changes in telework implementation rates before and after COVID-19. *Source* Survey on the state of telework in enterprises, JILPT, 2008, JILPT Panel Survey on the Impact of COVID-19 on Enterprise Management, JILPT, 2020–2022. Report on the results of the survey on diverse work style (telework), MGT, 2020

In the Tokyo metropolitan area, the participation rate in telework rapidly increased to 34.1% in 2020 and 42.1% in 2021 (MLIT 2022) (Fig. 2.2).[24]

Second, we can easily find differences by occupation. According to the '2021 Population Survey on Teleworkers', telework participation rates were high among researchers (64.1%), executives (51.6%), managers (51.1%), and professionals such as technical (49.8%), and clerical workers (32.4%). On the other hand, professionals in healthcare/law/education/finance (14.3%), service workers (6.2%), sales

[24] Only for hired employees, excluding self-employed/freelancers.

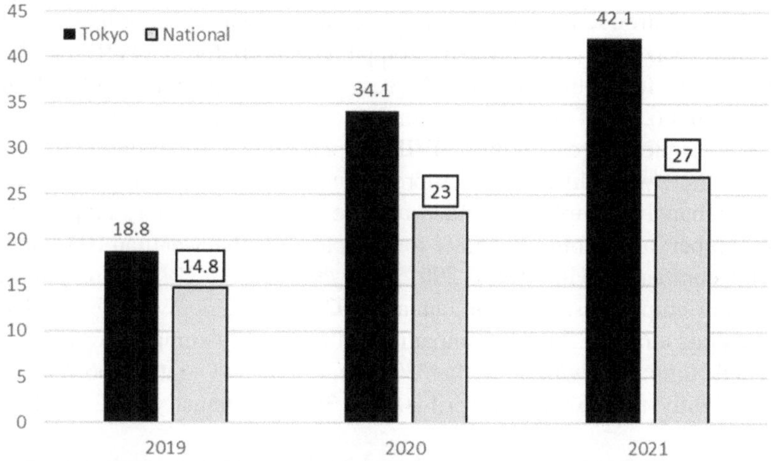

Fig. 2.3 The difference in telework implementation between Tokyo and the national average. *Source* Population Survey on Teleworkers, MLIT, 2019–2021

workers (4.7%), and safety and security workers (4.0%) had difficulty participating in telework (MLIT 2022).[25]

Third, this trend is confirmed by industry. According to the JILPT's survey in February 2020, the telework rate is low in all industries: construction (4.3%), manufacturing (3.4%), transport (0%), information and communications (5.0%), wholesale trade (8.5%), retail trade (0%), services (13.6%), medical, health care and welfare (0%), and accommodations, eating and drinking services (0%). However, in April 2020, the telework rate by industry dramatically surged: construction (65.2%), manufacturing (57.5%), transport (21.2%), information and communications (95.0%), wholesale trade (66.0%), retail trade (41.7%), services (81.8%), medical, health care, and welfare (0%), and accommodations, eating and drinking services (50%). It is clear that there are large differences in telework participation rates by industry. However, the most important point is how long the telework system has been maintained. What is clear is that telework has been introduced and established to some extent in all industries except for the medical welfare industry in the wake of the COVID-19 pandemic. After the peak in April 2020, the telework participation rate stabilized by industry. As of January 2022, the telework rate by industry was as follows: construction (30.4%), manufacturing (47.1%), transport (15.8%), information and communications (85.0%), wholesale trade (48.9%), retail trade (16.7%), services (54.5%), medical, health care, and welfare (0%), and accommodations, eating and drinking services (25%). One thing to note is the telework rate in the information and communications industry. The telework rate in the information and communications industry always exceeded 80% and sometimes reached 95% (JILPT 2022) (Fig. 2.3).

[25] Only for hired employees, excluding self-employed/freelancers.

Fourth, the introduction rate differs by company scale. According to a JILPT survey, there was little difference by company scale before COVID-19: 2.8% of companies with fewer than 100 employees, 5.8% of companies with 100 to 299 employees, and 6.3% of companies with 300 or more employees utilized telework. However, after the outbreak of the COVID-19 pandemic, the gap started to widen. In April 2020, there was a difference of approximately 33.6% points between companies with fewer than 100 employees and companies with 300 or more employees. The specific numbers are as follows: 45.8% for companies with fewer than 100 employees, 60.8% for companies with 100 to 299 employees, and 79.2% for companies with 300 or more employees. Even in January 2022, companies with fewer than 100 employees had a rate of 30.6%, companies with 100 to 299 employees had a rate of 43.3%, and companies with more than 300 employees had a rate of 66.7%. The gap widened slightly, from 33.6% in April 2020 to 36.1% in January 2022 (JILPT 2022) (Fig. 2.4).

In addition, the trend that the focus has shifted from mobile work to home-based telework is noteworthy. As mentioned above, telework can be classified into three categories: home-based telework, mobile work, and satellite offices. According to MIC's '2021 Communication usage trend survey (Businesses)', before the COVID-19 pandemic (in 2019), home-based telework accounted for 50.6%, mobile work accounted for 63.2%, and satellite offices accounted for 16.4%, with the percentage of mobile work being the highest. However, in 2021, with home-based telework at 91.5%, mobile work at 30.5%, and satellite offices at 15.2%, the proportion of mobile work decreased significantly, and the proportion of home-based telework soared (MIC 2021).

The Japanese government has implemented various policies to promote telework. However, most policies have failed to take root because of the resistance of customs and institutions in the labor market. In Japan, the COVID-19 pandemic

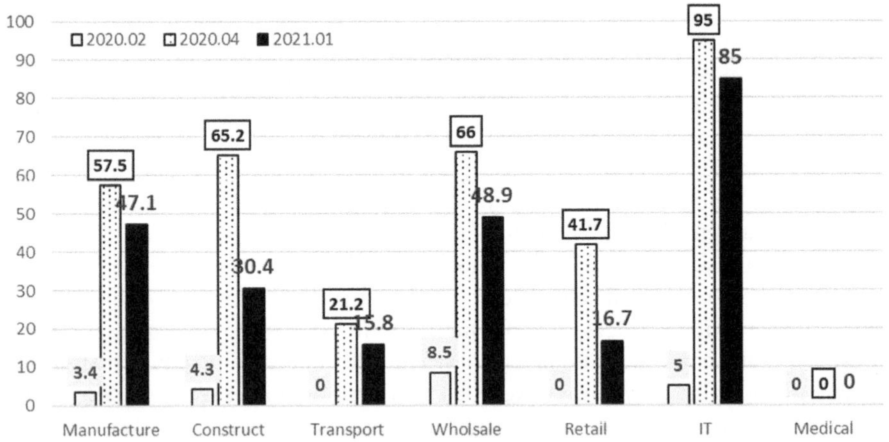

Fig. 2.4 Trends of telework by industry. *Source* JILPT panel survey on the impact of COVID-19 on enterprise management, JILPT, 2020–2022

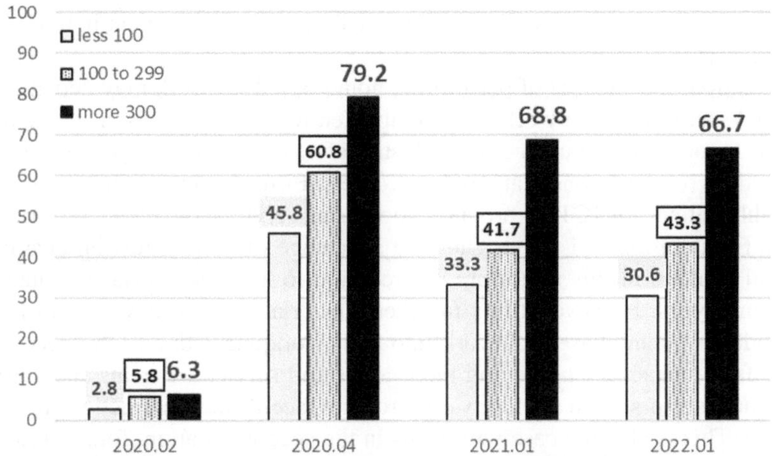

Fig. 2.5 The difference in telework implementation by company scale. *Source* JILPT panel survey on the impact of COVID-19 on enterprise management, JILPT, 2020–2022

accelerated telework practice. This means that the COVID-19 pandemic is the most important factor explaining the expansion of telework in Japan. In addition, we find some tendency that the implementation of telework depends on industry, occupation, company scale, and region. Therefore, researchers need to pay attention to the effects of those factors on telework implementation. In this context, this study examined the relationship between the above factors and telework implementation (Fig. 2.5).

2.3 Analytical Strategies

This study has two research concerns. First, it aims to examine what shaped access to home-based telework. To do so, we need to discuss the mechanisms by which people gained access to home-based telework during the COVID-19 pandemic. We assume that the structure of inequality determines who engaged with home-based telework during the COVID-19 pandemic because the chance to use telework is unequally distributed across individuals.

The human capital perspective helps us consider what shapes access to home-based telework. The SBTC hypothesis demonstrates the importance of computerization in increasing the wage inequality between highly skilled and unskilled workers. The insights of the SBTC hypothesis are applicable to inequality in the opportunity to engage in home-based telework during the COVID-19 pandemic because home-based telework requires workers to use computers and ICT. Highly skilled workers tend to use computers in their work more often than unskilled workers, and this was so even before the COVID-19 pandemic. Thus, we expect educational and occupational status to play a critical role in determining engagement in home-based telework across workers.

In addition, the chances of performing home-based telework may depend on the industrial sector in which workers are employed for the same reason as that argued from the human capital perspective. Industry refers to the type of goods and services produced by organizations that employ workers. Firms in several industrial sectors are highly reliant on ICT to produce goods and services for their customers and clients. Firms in the ICT sector can take advantage of their industrial characteristics, and workers in this sector are not required to have face-to-face contact with other employees. However, firms in other industrial sectors may face difficulties in introducing home-based telework into their workplaces due to the necessity of face-to-face contact for producing their goods and services. For instance, firms in care-related sectors, such as elderly care, require face-to-face interactions to provide that care. This is also the case with firms in the accommodation, food service, and transportation sectors.

Finally, we account for the financial cost of introducing home-based telework into an organization. During the COVID-19 pandemic, organizations needed to introduce home-based telework to reduce face-to-face contact among workers. To do this, organizations needed to cover the costs of buying computers, equipment for online meetings, or internet connections at home. However, firms may not have given all employees the opportunity to engage in home-based telework due to the inequality between regular and non-regular employees. As firms provide regular workers with opportunities to upgrade their skills and earn promotions on a long-term basis, we expect that firms would not hesitate to cover the costs of introducing home-based telework for regular workers. Conversely, firms generally hire non-regular workers on fixed-term or short-term contracts. Firms assign jobs that do not require firm-specific skills to non-regular employees. Given this context, we predict that there is inequality in home-based telework between regular and non-regular workers. Additionally, because profitability and financial ability differ between large and small firms, large firms may be more financially able to introduce home-based telework than small firms.

After examining inequality in access to home-based telework, as argued above, this study explores the consequences of people's engagement with home-based telework. We investigate how the introduction of home-based telework affects the number of work hours. Using panel data, we identify the causal effect of home-based telework on changing work hours. There are several possible scenarios in which the introduction of home-based telework would contribute to increasing or decreasing work hours. First, home-based telework may reduce work hours among workers in Japan. The virtue of hard work in Japanese organizational settings compels employees to work overtime. If a given employee or manager in the same section or department does overtime work in an office, other colleagues feel hesitant to leave the workplace earlier than those workers. In contrast, working from home using telecommunication devices may reduce workers' pressure to remain in the office until late at night.

Second, home-based telework may not contribute significantly to changing work hours. Home-based telework may increase the flexibility of the work schedule. For instance, some teleworkers can do household chores or take time to cook dinner during the lunch break. After preparing dinner, they can return to work very quickly. In addition, home-based teleworkers do not have to take time to commute between home and the workplace. They can reallocate the reduced commuting time to completing household chores. However, home-based telework does not necessarily reduce the working time itself because introducing telework does not necessarily change the number of tasks people have to do. Third, home-based telework may increase work hours. Home-based telework may obscure the distinction and boundary between home and the workplace. Although people stay home, they can work anytime using the ITC equipment. If many employees in Japan maintain the virtue of hard work during the COVID-19 pandemic, introducing telework may increase work hours among teleworkers.

Next, we focus on how people's job satisfaction and work-family conflicts depend on introducing telework. As argued above, introducing telework may have significant implications for balancing work and family demands. Teleworkers can increase the flexibility of the work-time schedule. By working from home using ICT devices, people can flexibly allocate their time to household chores and work during the day. In addition, because they do not need to take time to commute between home and the workplace, they can spend this time on other activities, such as doing housework or playing sports. The changing circumstances in people's schedules resulting from telework contribute to balancing work and family demands and increasing job satisfaction.

Conversely, home-based telework may worsen work conditions and increase the conflict between work and family. A critical reason is that introducing telework obscures the boundary between family and work domains. For example, suppose a situation where teleworkers have to work overtime. Because they are busy with their work schedule, they cannot find time to do household chores, although they stay home. Moreover, workers cannot escape thinking about their jobs even when staying home. Given these considerations, we empirically address the issues of whether introducing telework during the COVID-19 pandemic improves or worsens the balance between work and family domains and workers' subjective well-being.

2.4 Data, Methods, and Variables

2.4.1 Data and Methods

In this study, we derived data from the Survey on Work and Life under COVID-19 (WLCV survey) conducted in November 2020 and May 2021. We also engaged in designing this survey. The survey sample was randomly chosen from a list of registered individuals in the Japan Research Center (JRC) Corporation, one of Japan's most well-known research companies. The sample was restricted to individuals aged 25 to 44 with a spouse and more than one child, mainly because this research project focused on how the COVID-19 pandemic affected family life situations among couples with children. The investigators mailed the questionnaire to the selected 1,000 individuals, and 626 individuals responded to the survey in November 2020. We later conducted a second wave of the survey targeting the 626 individuals who responded to the first wave. Finally, 503 individuals responded to the second wave of the survey. The response rates of the two surveys were 62.6 and 80.4%, respectively.

A strength of this survey is that it measured work and family situations from January 2020 to May 2021 over five different time points. We view January 2020 as the time before the COVID-19 pandemic occurred in Japan. May 2020 was when schools were closed, and the government requested workers stay home to work if possible. November 2020 was the time when the first wave of the WLCV survey was implemented. January 2021 was the time when the state of emergency was declared again due to the increase in the number of COVID-19 patients. In May 2021, the second wave of the WLCV survey was undertaken.

Let us explain the extent to which the observations of the WLCV survey represent the situation of the whole population in Japan. The WLCV survey utilized the list of individuals registered in the JRC, which originated with those who responded to questionnaire surveys implemented by the research company in the past. The surveys used the housing map data to randomly select households nationwide in Japan, and individuals were then selected from within the chosen households. The surveys also requested the respondents to participate in other surveys, and those who agreed to do so were added to a list of registered individuals in the JRC. Therefore, we cannot strictly state that we chose our sample randomly from a whole population in Japan for the WLCV survey.

However, it was also challenging to implement the systemic sampling procedure using a list of resident registration records in 2020 due to the COVID-19 pandemic. We had no choice but to use a list of registered individuals held by a research company. Several research companies keep lists of registered individuals who can respond to questions in a survey. These firms usually invited people to participate in a survey on their websites to compose their list. Such a sampling procedure would probably produce serious bias in the distributions of some observed variables. For this reason, the data set derived from the WLCV survey is more representative than data based on web-based surveys targeting people on the internet.

We checked the discrepancies in demographic characteristics between the data of the WLCV survey and the data of other surveys using systemic sampling procedures.[26] We also used the Social Stratification and Mobility (SSM) survey conducted in 2015 because it is one of the well-known surveys that randomly sampled individuals nationwide in Japan. We also restricted samples to individuals aged 25 to 44 who were married and had children in the SSM survey data. The results by region show that compared with the SSM, the WLCV included more individuals living in Kanto and Kansai and fewer living in Hokkaido, Tohoku, and Kyushu. In the SSM, 30% lived in Kanto, but in the WLCV, 36% did. 13% of individuals sampled in the SSM resided in Kyushu, and the figure was 11% in the WLCV. As the original sample

[26] This analysis is based on the data from the first wave of the WLCV survey.

was randomly chosen from the housing map data, there were smaller discrepancies in place of residence among respondents. Regarding educational attainment, more individuals had attained university education in the WLCV sample (36%) than in the SSM sample (31%). Fewer individuals had completed middle school or high school in the WLCV (28%) than in the SSM (37%). Hence, we found a relatively large gap in the share of people with lower education between these two surveys. We need to account for this bias when considering the results of our study.

This study focuses on inequality in access to home-based telework and the consequences of telework on work hours and workers' subjective well-being. The number of samples differs depending on the research theme. Regarding access to telework, we applied the event history model, and we used samples who responded to both waves of the survey as well as those who responded to the first wave but not the second wave. The event history model allows us to include those who dropped out of the panel survey and to treat them as right-censored cases. Concerning work hours, we also used all samples who responded to both waves and to only the first wave because each survey measured situations of employment at multiple time points. With respect to job satisfaction and work-family conflict, we need to restrict samples to those who responded to both the first and the second wave of the WLCV survey because each survey measured these conditions at the time of survey implementation.

We provide details for the variables used in the multivariate analysis in this study. Table 2.1 lists the descriptive statistics used for the multivariate analyses. The number of samples differs depending on the statistical models used in this study. Regarding the event history model predicting access to telework, the unit of observation was set to periods rather than individuals. Because the WLCV survey measured work conditions at different time points within the same year, we examined the timing of the transition into telework at a monthly level. The number of cases in the variables used for the event history model expanded to more than 6000 cases. In the analyses on weekly work hours, we used information on work conditions measured at five different time points. The number of cases used for the analysis predicting work hours was 2103. Finally, we used the WLCV data to investigate the effects of home-based telework on workers' subjective well-being: job satisfaction and work-family conflicts. These variables were measured in two different time periods when this panel survey was undertaken: November 2020 and May 2021. The number of samples thus became 790.

To investigate inequality in access to telework and the consequences of telework, we employed several statistical models. We used the logit model to predict access to telework in January 2020 before the COVID-19 pandemic occurred. Moreover, we applied the complementary log–log model to predict the timing of telework participation. The complementary log–log model (clog-log) is formulated in the following manner:

$$clog - log = \log(-\log(1 - p)),\ \text{where } \rho \text{ denotes the probability of } y = 1 \quad (2.1)$$

Thus, the clog-log transformation yields the logarithm of the negated logarithm of the probability of event nonoccurrence (Singer & Willet, 2014). Many researchers

Table 2.1 Descriptive statistics used for the multivariate analyses

	N	Mean	S.D
Dependent outcomes			
Work at home	6,110	0.016	
Weekly work hours	2,103	34.854	15.900
Job satisfaction			
Wage	788	2.138	1.208
Employment stability	790	2.643	1.076
Job content	790	2.633	1.008
Work environment	790	2.558	1.064
Work hours	788	2.607	1.116
Relation with colleagues	790	2.718	1.055
Work-family conflict			
Work-to-family conflict1	790	2.115	0.970
Work-to-family conflict2	790	2.073	0.952
Family-to-work conflict1	790	1.810	0.828
Family-to-work conflict2	790	1.768	0.798
Independent variables			
(Continuous Variable)			
Time since January 2020	6,110	7.281	4.956
Age	473	38.161	4.439
(Discrete Variable)			
Emergency state	6,110	0.070	
Female	473	0.493	
Education			
High school or less	473	0.296	
Post-secondary vocational	473	0.211	
Low tertiary	473	0.116	
University or higher	473	0.376	
Employment status			
Regular employment	6,110	0.532	
Non-regular employment	6,110	0.369	
Self-employment	6,110	0.099	
Industry			
Manufacturing/construction	6,110	0.249	
Unskilled service	6,110	0.278	
Professional service	6,110	0.201	
Medicine and welfare	6,110	0.191	
Public and others	6,110	0.081	
Firm size			

(continued)

Table 2.1 (continued)

	N	Mean	S.D
Small firms	6,110	0.302	
Medium-sized firms	6,110	0.293	
Large and public firms	6,110	0.405	
Occupation			
Professional/managers	6,110	0.329	
Clerical	6,110	0.160	
Sales/service	6,110	0.303	
Manual	6,110	0.208	

have used the logit link to estimate the discrete-time hazard model due to the convenience and popularity of logistic regression. Moreover, the complementary log–log model has a fundamental advantage over the logit model in discrete-time event history analysis. The clog-log model has a proportional hazards assumption but not a proportional odds assumption, as in the logit model. For this reason, we also decided to use the clog-log transformation in the event history analysis on telework participation.

In addition, regarding the consequences of home-based telework, we used the fixed-effects regression model to predict weekly work hours and the conflicts between work and family demands. The advantage of the fixed-effects regression model is that we can estimate the causal effect of introducing home-based telework on several outcomes of interest, such as work hours, job satisfaction, and accommodating work and family life.

The formula of the fixed-effects regression model is as follows:

$$y_{it} = \mu_t + \beta x_{it} + \alpha_i + \varepsilon_{it} \tag{2.2}$$

We have a set of individuals ($i = 1, \ldots, n$), each of whom is measured at two or more time points ($t = 1, \ldots, T$). We let y_{it} be the dependent variable. We have a set of predictor variables that vary over time, represented by the vector $\mathrm{x_{it}}$. μ_t is an intercept that may be different over time. This equation has two error terms: α_i and ε_{it}. ε_{it} differs across individuals at each time point, but α_i varies only across individuals, not over time. When we focus on the difference between the values of variables at each time point and average values within individuals across the time points, we can eliminate α_i from the equation as specified in (3) (Allison, 2009).

$$y_{it} - \overline{y}_i = (x_{it} - \overline{x}_i)\beta + (\varepsilon_{it} - \overline{\varepsilon}_i), \qquad \text{where } (\alpha_i - \overline{\alpha}_i) = 0 \tag{2.3}$$

The WLCV survey measured the length of work hours at five different time points and the work-family conflict at two time points. We can thus apply the fixed-effects regression model to these panel data and estimate the causal effect of introducing home-based telework on reducing work hours and improving the balance between work and family demands.

2.4.2 Variables

We provide details for the variables used in the multivariate analysis in this study. We used several dependent outcomes: engagement with home-based telework, work hours, job satisfaction, and work-family conflict. Regarding home-based telework, the WLCV survey measured whether respondents were working at home at five different time points: January, May, and November 2020 and January and May 2021. For individuals who worked at home at all five different time points, the variable of home-based telework was coded as one, and it was set to zero for all others. Work hours were treated as a continuous variable. The WLCV survey measured the six items of job satisfaction: wage, employment stability, the content of a job, work environment, work hours, and relationships with other colleagues. To do so, we used a five-point scale from satisfied to dissatisfied. We also employed the conflict between work and family demands. There are two types of work-family conflict. The first typology assumes that work demands cause conflict in the family sphere (WFC, hereafter). The second typology assumes the opposite situation: family demands cause conflict in the work sphere (FWC, hereafter). Each typology has two questions.[27] The survey adopts a four-point scale in response to the questions, ranging from applicable to not applicable.

The independent variables include gender, age, education, employment status, industry, organizational size, and occupational status. The work-related variables used in this study were measured in January 2020. These variables include employment status, industry, firm size, and occupational status. The place of residence in this study was measured at the time of the survey. Age is treated as a continuous variable. Education is split into four categories: high school or less, postsecondary vocational school, lower tertiary school, such as a two-year junior college, and a four-year university or higher. The industry of the employer is divided into five categories: manufacturing, construction, and agriculture, which is set as the reference category; the unskilled service sector (retail, food services, and tourism); the professional services sector (accounting, information technology, law, consulting, finance, and research); the health, medicine, and care-related sector; and the public services and other services sectors. Firm size has three categories: small (fewer than 29 employees), medium (more than 30 and fewer than 299 employees), and large (more than 300 employees), and public. The place of residence is dichotomized: large city and other.[5)]

[27] IN the WFC, the survey measured the extent to which respondents could not spend enough time with their family due to busy work schedules and the extent to which respondents could not stop thinking about work even when at home. In the FWC, it measured the extent to which the respondents could not allocate their time to work due to family affairs and the extent to which the respondents were so tired from housework that they did not feel like doing their job.

2.5 Home-Based Telework During the COVID-19 Pandemic

2.5.1 Descriptive Statistics

Figure 2.6 presents the proportion of teleworkers to all workers in 2020 and 2021, using the data derived from the Survey on Work and Life under COVID-19 (the WLCV survey). The results show that in January 2020, before the COVID-19 pandemic, only 5% of workers performed telework at home. In May 2021, during the state of emergency period, the teleworkers' proportion increased to more than 20%. After the declaration of the state of emergency ended, the proportion declined to less than 10% in November 2020. The 2020 WLCV survey also asked teleworkers other questions concerning home-based telework.

Figure 2.7 indicates the extent to which teleworkers felt satisfied with the circumstances of doing telework at home. More than half of teleworkers were satisfied with home-based telework, while 20% were dissatisfied. The WLCV survey also measured whether teleworkers received any support from their employers when they started teleworking at home. Only 22% of teleworkers received support from their employers when starting telework. 64% did not gain support from their employers. Furthermore, this survey asked teleworkers whether they hoped to do telework after the COVID-19 pandemic. Less than half of teleworkers (46%) expected to do telework, and 51% did not expect to.

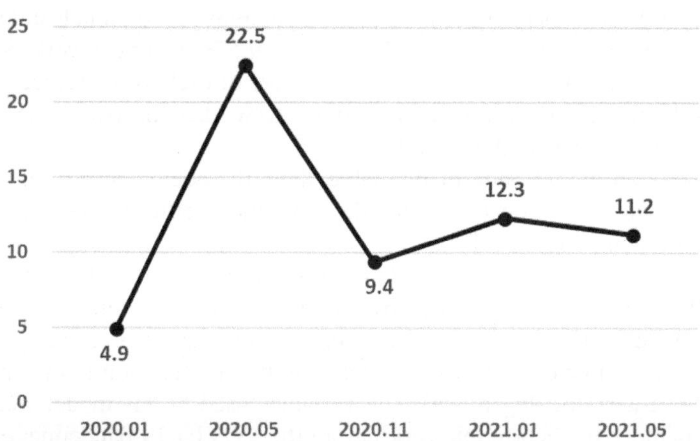

Fig. 2.6 The proportion of teleworkers to all workers in 2020 and 2021

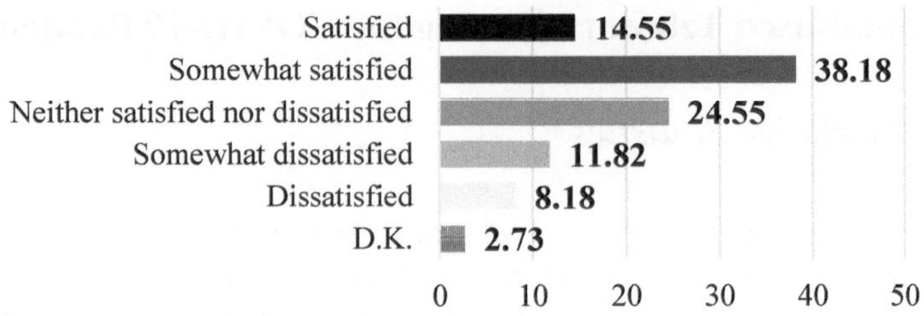

Fig. 2.7 Level of satisfaction with home-based telework (N = 110)

2.5.2 *Inequality in Access to Telework*

Table 2.2 presents the inequality in access to telework, estimated by the multivariate analyses. The left side of this table shows the results of the logistic regression model predicting home-based telework in January 2020, before the COVID-19 pandemic occurred in Japan. The model included several socioeconomic variables as predictors for explaining access to telework. We did not find any significant effects of socioeconomic variables, such as education and occupation, on access to telework in January 2020, except for employment status. We see that the self-employed were more likely to do telework than non-regular workers. There was also a significant difference at a 10% level between clerical and manual workers in home-based telework. We predicted the telework probabilities based on the logit model estimates. Before the COVID-19 pandemic, 19.5% of self-employed individuals did telework, while only 2.2% of regular workers did. A total of 9.5% of clerical workers engaged in teleworking, but only 2.9% of manual workers did telework. Hence, based on the results, home-based telework was restricted to workers in specific occupational situations before the COVID-19 pandemic.

The results on the left side of this table show the coefficient estimated by the logit model. The results on the right side show the coefficients estimated by the complementary log–log model.

Table 2.2 on the right side presents the results of telework engagement during the COVID-19 pandemic, estimated by the event history model. Samples used in the model were restricted to individuals who did not telework in January 2020. We used the discrete-time event history model, and the link function in this model was the complementary log–log model. The variables used in this model were almost the same as those predicting telework before the COVID-19 pandemic, except for the timing of the event occurrence. We found remarkable divergences in the results between the two models. In the event history model, we controlled for the timing of the event occurrence using two variables: the time elapsed since the start of the COVID-19 pandemic and the timing of the emergency state declaration. We see that during the period of the first emergency state declaration, that is, May 2020, workers were more likely to introduce telework. After controlling for the effects of the timing of the event occurrence, there were significant variations in the introduction of telework by socioeconomic status.

Table 2.2 The results predicting access to telework before and during the COVID-19 pandemic

	Telework before the pandemic		Telework during the pandemic	
	Coef	S.E	Coef	S.E
Time since January 2020			0.337**	0.083
Period of emergency state			6.988**	0.847
Gender	0.857	0.631	0.427	0.324
Age	−0.055	0.059	0.031	0.025
Education (reference: high school or less)				
Post-secondary vocational school	−0.076	0.727	0.191	0.447
Junior college	−0.880	1.223	0.423	0.454
University or higher	0.679	0.647	1.003**	0.314
Employment status (reference: non-regular employment)				
Regular employment	−0.196	0.760	1.269**	0.422
Self-employment	2.496**	0.792	1.192*	0.567
Industry (reference: manufacturing and construction)				
Unskilled service	−0.506	0.887	0.197	0.345
Professional service	0.444	0.713	0.760*	0.295
Medicine and welfare	−1.001	1.213	−1.624*	0.631
Public and others	0.330	0.979	-0.044^{+}	0.388
Firm size (reference: small)				
Medium	−0.664	0.792	0.611	0.385
Large and public	−0.745	0.772	1.127**	0.353
Occupation (reference: manual)				
Professional/ managerial	−0.072	0.863	0.351	0.363
Clerical	1.558^{+}	0.914	0.241	0.421
Sales/service	0.462	0.903	−0.216	0.413
Constant	−2.392	2.494	−13.789**	1.645
N	473		6110	
X^2	40.04**		287.18**	
Pseudo R^2	0.242			

Note $^{+}p < 0.10$ $^{*}p < 0.05$ $^{**}p < 0.01$

Gender and age were not significantly related to introducing home-based telework during the COVID-19 pandemic. To consider the results of gender in greater detail, we compared the gender difference in telework before and after controlling for the effects of socioeconomic conditions. Without controlling for educational and occupational status, women were less likely to perform home-based telework than men. However, the significant gender inequality vanished after controlling for the effects of employment and occupational status. This means that men were more likely to do telework than women because more men were concentrated in the regular employment sector and engaged in occupations with higher status than women.

2.5.3 The Consequences of Home-Based Telework

In this section, we focus on the consequences of home-based telework. Home-based telework may change how people work. Many workers employed in an organization usually do their jobs in offices or workplaces, away from home. This situation generates a clear boundary between home and the workplace. Employees in a workplace cannot perform household chores at the same time. However, home-based telework allows people to undertake both their jobs and household chores in a flexible manner. In addition, people do not need to take the time to commute between home and the workplace. Home-based telework may thus improve the balance between work and family demands.

To consider the outcome that resulted from home-based telework, we investigate how introducing home-based telework changed work hours over time during the COVID-19 pandemic. The WLCV survey used in this analysis measured several dimensions of work and employment among respondents at five different time points: January, May, and November in 2020 and January and May in 2021. We employed this information and created a data set that is suitable for panel data analysis. To control for the unobserved heterogeneity across individuals, we applied the fixed-effect regression model. By using this model, we can identify whether introducing home-based telework significantly changed work hours within individuals over time.

Table 2.3 presents the results predicting work hours using the fixed-effect regression models. In Model 1, we included whether people worked at home. We did not find any significant influence of home-based telework on work hours. In Model 2, we added the interaction term of work at home and gender to Model 1. Because we used the fixed-effect regression model, we did not need to control the additive effect of gender in this model. We found both additive and interaction effects of home-based telework and gender in this model. Men who performed telework significantly reduced their work hours. However, female home-based teleworkers did not reduce their work hours. In Model 3, after controlling for each time point, the additive effect of home-based telework became insignificant, while this interaction term with gender remained significant at the 10% level. The results indicate that many workers uniformly declined their work hours in May 2020, the emergency state period. In Model 4, we controlled the occupation-related variables. The significant effect of the interaction term of home-based telework with gender vanished. Summarizing this result, workers uniformly experienced declining work hours during the emergency state period, and introducing home-based telework during this period did not have any causal effect on reducing the length of work hours among men or women.

Table 2.3 The fixed-effect regression models predicting work hours

	Model 1		Model 2	
	Coef.	s.e.	Coef.	s.e.
Work at home	−1.234	0.816	−2.502*	1.065
Interaction term between work at home and female dummy			3.060+	1.655
Constant	35.007**	0.195	34.999**	0.195
Number of observations	2103		2103	
Number of individuals	506		506	
ρ	0.792		0.794	
R^2	0.002		0.016	
F	2.29		2.85+	
	Model 3		Model 4	
	Coef.	s.e.	Coef.	s.e.
Work at home	−1.105	1.094	−1.058	1.095
Interaction term between work at home and female dummy	2.943+	1.645	2.698	1.647
Time (Reference: January 2020)				
May 2020	−2.641**	0.543	−2.669**	0.542
November 2020	−0.585	0.516	−0.650	0.515
January 2021	−0.744	0.557	−0.863	0.559
May 2021	−0.694	0.557	−0.867	0.561
Employment status (Reference: Regular employment)				
Non-regular employment			−4.026*	1.588
Self-employment			1.534	3.083
Firm size (Reference: Small)				
Medium			−0.400	1.701
Large and public			0.133	1.995
Industry (Reference: Manufacturing and construction)				
Unskilled service			−1.790	2.262
Professional service			0.240	2.164
Medicine and welfare			1.157	2.965
Public and others			3.068	2.704
Occupation (Reference: Professional/Managerial)				
Clerical			0.213	1.910
Sales/service			0.831	1.178
Manual			1.887	1.170
Constant	35.771**	0.373	36.381**	2.180

(continued)

Table 2.3 (continued)

	Model 3		Model 4	
	Coef.	s.e.	Coef.	s.e.
Number of observations	2103		2103	
Number of individuals	506		506	
ρ	0.796		0.766	
R^2	0.000		0.234	
F	5.47**		3.04**	

Note $^{+}p < 0.10$ $^{*}p < 0.05$ $^{**}p < 0.01$

We then explored whether and how home-based telework changed people's satisfaction with their job and work circumstances. Although home-based telework did not contribute substantially to reducing work hours, it may have improved people's satisfaction with jobs because telework may help people accommodate conflict between work and family demands. The WLCV survey measured the six items of job satisfaction at two different time points: November 2020 and May 2021. The six items included satisfaction with wages, employment stability, work content, work environment, work hours, and relationships with other colleagues. We also applied the fixed-effect regression model to the panel data to control for the unobserved heterogeneity across individuals. We used all six variables about job satisfaction as the dependent outcomes. We had the two models for the analyses. In Model 1, we included home-based teleworking as an independent variable without any controls. In Model 2, we added the interaction term of telework with gender to the first model to check whether the effect of home-based telework differs between men and women.

Table 2.4 lists the results predicting the six variables of job satisfaction. In Model 1, none of the six job satisfaction variables depended on home-based telework. Overall, home-based telework did not increase or decrease job satisfaction. In Model 2, the result of satisfaction with work hours showed a significant interaction effect of telework and gender, while the results of other satisfaction variables did not have such an interaction effect. We found that male workers gained increased satisfaction with work hours through telework, but we could not find this pattern for female workers. The left side of Table 2.5 presents how satisfaction with work hours depends on home-based telework with other occupational characteristics controlled. The result indicates that the additive and interaction effects of home-based telework and gender remain significant even after controlling for other occupational characteristics.

It is very important to consider why male workers experienced higher satisfaction with work hours, although telework did not increase their work hours. We can discuss several reasons for this. First, teleworkers do not have to take time to commute between home and the workplace. The introduction of telework enables workers to spend this time on other activities, such as doing household chores or other leisure activities. Second, teleworkers can manage their time for paid work and unpaid housework in a flexible manner. For example, during lunch breaks, they can go to a supermarket to buy ingredients for dinner. After lunch, they can start cooking

Table 2.4 The fixed-effect regression models predicting the six dimensions of job satisfaction

	Wage		Employment stability		Content of a job	
	Coef	S.E	Coef	S.E	Coef	S.E
<Model 1>						
Work at home	−0.042	0.198	−0.292	0.189	−0.167	0.192
Constant	2.151**	0.031	2.672**	0.029	2.655**	0.030
N of Obs	873		874		874	
N of Groups	511		510		510	
F	0.04		2.38		0.76	
<Model 2>						
Work at home	0.143	0.260	−0.429+	0.248	−0.071	0.251
Interaction with gender	−0.443	0.402	0.329	0.384	−0.229	0.389
Constant	2.152**	0.031	2.671	0.029	2.656**	0.030
N of Obs	873		874		874.000	
N of Groups	511		510		510.000	
F	0.63		1.55		0.55	

	Work environment		Work hours		Relations with colleagues	
	Coef	S.E	Coef	S.E	Coef	S.E
<Model 1>						
Work at home	0.083	0.205	0.167	0.202	0.000	0.185
Constant	2.534**	0.032	2.582**	0.031	2.714**	0.029
N of Obs	874		872		874	
N of Groups	510		510		510	
F	0.16		0.68		0.00	
<Model 2>						
Work at home	0.000	0.269	0.643*	0.262	0.071	0.242
Interaction with gender	0.200	0.417	−1.143**	0.406	−0.171	0.375
Constant	2.533	0.032	2.584**	0.031	2.714**	0.029
N of Obs	874		872		874	
N of Groups	510		510		510	
F	0.20		4.31*		0.10	

Note $^{+}p < 0.10$ $^{*}p < 0.05$ $^{**}p < 0.01$

Table 2.5 The fixed-effect regression model predicting work hour satisfaction and family-to-work conflict

	Work hour satisfaction		Family-to-work conflict	
	Coef	S.E	Coef	S.E
Work at home	0.571*	0.267	0.357⁺	0.185
Interaction term between work at home and female dummy	−1.164**	0.423	0.061	0.047
Time	−0.003	0.053		
Employment status (reference: regular employment)				
Mom-regular employment	−0.094	0.240	0.588**	0.213
Self-employment	0.766	0.529	0.329	0.439
Industry (reference: manufacturing and construction)				
Unskilled service	0.058	0.323	−0.371	0.287
Professional service	0.599*	0.303	−0.315	0.269
Medicine and welfare	0.299	0.450	−0.112	0.401
Public and others	0.542	0.372	−0.285	0.331
Firm size (reference: small)				
Medium	0.220	0.266	0.279	0.226
Large and public	0.342	0.302	0.239	0.259
Occupation (reference: professional/managerial)				
Clerical	0.241	0.281	0.039	0.244
Sales/service	0.191	0.169	0.070	0.149
Manual	0.256	0.162	0.152	0.142
Constant	1.935**	0.320	1.500**	0.281
Number of observations	863		874	
Number of individuals	506		508	
ρ(rho)	0.717		0.628	
R^2	0.000		0.000	
F	1.62⁺		1.31	

Note $^{+}p < 0.10$ $^{*}p < 0.05$ $^{**}p < 0.01$

something. After cutting vegetables and meat, they stop cooking and return to work. In the evening, they can start cooking again.[28]

However, home-based telework does not always have a positive influence on boosting workers' subjective well-being. The right side of Table 2.5 shows the effect of home-based telework on family-to-work conflict with the same occupational characteristics controlled. Family-to-work conflict measures the extent to which workers

[28] An example about this issue: Newspaper article: 'Japan study shows huge gap in child care burden among female and male doctors' The Mainichi, May 22, 2022, 'https://mainichi.jp/english/articles/20220520/p2a/00m/0na/025000c'.

cannot take enough time for their work because there are many things to do in housework or other family affairs. Even after controlling for the same occupational characteristics as in the model predicting satisfaction with work hours, home-based telework had a significant effect on the family-to-work conflict at a 10% level. We did not find any gender difference in this association (results not shown). Hence, home-based telework increased family-to-work conflict rather than decreasing it. Because teleworkers stay home to work, we assume that the boundary between work and family becomes blurred and obscured. As they work at home, some family affairs, such as childcare or household chores, may hinder teleworkers from concentrating on their jobs.

2.6 Discussion and Conclusion

The history of home-based telework extends over more than 30 years. For a long time, even though organizations and governments have made plans for the spread of home-based telework, the coverage of home-based telework has been lower than the early forecasts predicted. Rather, home-based telework dramatically expanded after the beginning of the COVID-19 pandemic. In this context, this study examines the reasons and results of telework practice using the WLCV survey. The results of this study can be summarized as follows.

First, the number of teleworkers increased after the start of the COVID-19 pandemic but to a limited extent. In May 2020, the percentage of teleworkers reached 23.7%; however, 6 months later in November, the percentage decreased to 9.8%. From this result, we can confirm that pandemic-induced telework is a social phenomenon in the COVID-19 pandemic era.

Second, highly skilled workers can easily work at home. According to previous research, home-based telework is directly related to the availability of ICT. Therefore, compared to manual workers, who rely heavily on work facilities to perform their tasks, professionals and managers have a much higher probability of engaging in home-based telework. Consequently, for those who have the ability to work with ICT and who can complete their jobs using a personal computer anywhere, home-based telework is a good choice to avoid the risk of infection with COVID-19.

Third, regarding the availability of ICT, disparities between industrial sectors have emerged. Compared with the manufacturing, construction, and agriculture sectors, the professional service sector has a high telework participation rate. This is because it is easy for workers in the professional service sector to work at home relative to workers who need physical access to the equipment in their workplace. We also explored how the intersection between occupation and industry shaped access to telework. In the manufacturing sector, occupation plays a role in increasing access to telework. In contrast, the professional service sector helps more workers engage in teleworking, regardless of their jobs. This result provides us with insights into the importance of industry in generating inequality in telework.

Fourth, considering the average learning capability of workers, highly educated workers tend to engage in telework, as we expected. This is a reasonable finding, but it also has many implications for the study of inequality and stratification. Considering the reasons for the increase in home-based telework during the COVID-19 pandemic, we find that engagement in telework is directly linked to inequality in infection risk. Suppose that workers are infected with COVID-19 while commuting or at the workplace. These workers may see a decrease in their wages due to their sickness or, in the worst case, lose their jobs. Given the significant disparity in access to telework by the level of education, education has played a more distinctive role in generating and reinforcing inequality in life chances across individuals during the pandemic than it did in the past.

Fifth, telework in itself restrictively affects working conditions. Telework has not played a substantial role in reducing working hours regardless of gender. If anything, telework increases gender inequality in job satisfaction. For male workers, telework positively increases job satisfaction, but female workers who engage in telework experience a decrease in job satisfaction. Most previous research has reported the same results as our findings.

In summary, even though telework has spread during the COVID-19 pandemic, we cannot rule out the possibility that this is a temporary phenomenon. Most companies and organizations introduced telework as a temporary measure. Given that the Japanese government has tried to spread telework for a long time and that the COVID-19 pandemic has been a good opportunity to implement a telework policy, this low rate of telework introduction is an interesting point in the field of social inequality.

Additionally, our results suggest that inequality in telework engagement reflects the existing inequality structure and has helped maintain the status quo for social inequality. In the pandemic era, telework is an important safety net for preventing infection. Thus, inequality in access to telework can be viewed as a component of the newly emerging inequality in infection risk. Based on previous studies, we need to recognize that telework does not always improve working conditions, work–life balance, or work satisfaction. Nevertheless, if traditional inequality structures, such as occupational status, education, region, industry, and employment type, have a strong influence on participation in telework, telework may have become a new source of inequality and social stratification during this pandemic of a new infectious disease.

More importantly, this study supports gender inequality in telework practice. According to our findings, while male workers feel an increase in job satisfaction, female workers suffer from telework. Regarding the reason for this phenomenon, it is a reasonable interpretation that when female workers implement telework, cultural and social pressure is imposed on them to do housework more affirmatively just because they are at home.

Given our research findings and their implications, in follow-up research, we need to examine how and to what extent telework creates and reinforces inequality in a different dimension in the long run after the end of the COVID-19 pandemic. In 2020 and 2021, most companies implemented telework forcedly regardless of their actual demand and without enough preparation. Currently, some companies have stopped telework, while others are trying to expand it. To understand the actual effect of telework on social inequality, scholars need to examine the long-term effects of telework after the pandemic.

In telework practice, telework is just a tool. Tools cannot alleviate or remedy our problems. Social inequality and working conditions are no exceptions. If we do not take action to reduce social inequality and deliberate how we can utilize telework to reduce social inequality and improve working conditions, telework will reproduce current problems or make things worse. Researchers, politicians, capitalists, workers, and unions need to start action to make telework a tool for the reduction in inequality and improvement in working conditions.

Finally, we note the limitations of this article. First, the number of observations is relatively small, and the sample is restricted to those aged 25 to 44 with a spouse and more than one child. Therefore, it is difficult to argue that the results of this research are valid for all workers in the Japanese labor market. Second, home-based telework is a small component of all telework, so follow-up research needs to extend the scope of telework from home-based telework to other types of telework.

References

Adams-Prassl, A., Boneva, T., Golin, M., & Rauh, C. (2020). Inequality in the impact of the coronavirus shock: Evidence from real time surveys. *Journal of Public Economics, 189*, 104245.

Agba, A. O., Ocheni, S. I., & Agba, M. S. (2020). COVID-19 and the world of work dynamics: A critical review. *Journal of Educational and Social Research, 10*(5), 119–219.

Allison, P. D. (2009). *Fixed effects regression models*. 2455 Teller Road, Thousand Oaks, California 91320, United States of America: SAGE Publications, Inc.

Autor, D. H., Levy, F., & Murnane, R. J. (2003). Skill demand, inequality, and computerization: Connecting the dots. In D. K. Ginther, M. Zavodny, & L. H. Foley (Eds.), *Technology, growth, and the labor market* (pp. 107–129). Boston, MA, US: Springer.

Bailey, D. E., & Kurland, N. B. (2002). A review of telework research: Findings, new directions, and lessons for the study of modern work. *Journal of Organizational Behavior: The International Journal of Industrial, Occupational and Organizational Psychology and Behavior, 23*(4), 383–400.

Baruch, Y., & Nicholson, N. (1997). Home, sweet work: Requirements for effective home working. *Journal of general management, 23*(2), 15–30.

Bélanger, F. (1999). Workers' propensity to telecommute: An empirical study. *Information & Management, 35*(3), 139–153.

Bick, A., Blandin, A., & Mertens, K. (2020). *Work from home after the COVID-19 outbreak*.

Belzunegui-Eraso, A., & Erro-Garcés, A. (2020). Teleworking in the context of the Covid-19 crisis. *Sustainability, 12*(9), 3662.

Boell, S. K., Cecez-Kecmanovic, D., & Campbell, J. (2016). Telework paradoxes and practices: The importance of the nature of work. *New Technology, Work and Employment, 31*(2), 114–131.

Brynjolfsson, E., Horton, J. J., Ozimek, A., Rock, D., Sharma, G., & TuYe, H. Y. (2020). COVID-19 and remote work: An early look at US data (No. w27344). *National Bureau of Economic Research*.

Card, D., & DiNardo, J. E. (2002). Technology growth and the labor market technology and U.S. wage inequality: A brief look. In D. K. Ginther, M. Zavodny, & L. H. Foley (Eds.), *Technology, growth, and the labor market* (pp. 131–160). Boston, MA, US: Springer.

Del Boca, D., Oggero, N., Profeta, P., & Rossi, M. (2020). Women's and men's work, housework and childcare, before and during COVID-19. *Review of Economics of the Household, 18*(4), 1001–1017.

Diab-Bahman, R., & Al-Enzi, A. (2020). The impact of COVID-19 pandemic on conventional work settings. *International Journal of Sociology and Social Policy, 40*(2), 909–927.

Di Martino, V., & Wirth, L. (1990). Telework: A new way of working and living. *International Labour Review, 129*, 529–554.

Dingel, J. I., & Neiman, B. (2020). How many jobs can be done at home? *Journal of Public Economics, 189*, 104235.

Donnelly, N., & Proctor-Thomson, S. B. (2015). Disrupted work: Home-based teleworking (HbTW) in the aftermath of a natural disaster. *New Technology, Work and Employment, 30*(1), 47–61.

Elldér, E. (2019). Who is eligible for telework? Exploring the fast-growing acceptance of and ability to telework in Sweden, 2005–2006 to 2011–2014. *Social Sciences, 8*(7), 200.

Erikson, R., & Goldthorpe, J. G. (1992). *The constant flux: A study of class mobility in industrial societies*. Oxford University Press.

Eurofound. (2020). *Living, working and COVID-19: First findings April 2020*.

Frolick, M. N., Wilkes, R. B., & Urwiler, R. (1993). Telecommuting as a workplace alternative: An identification of significant factors in American firms' determination of work-at-home policies. *The Journal of Strategic Information Systems, 2*(3), 206–220.

Gareis, K., Hüsing, T., & Mentrup, A. (2004). What drives eWork? An exploration into determinants of eWork uptake in Europe. In *9th international telework workshop* (pp. 6–9).

Gilbert, M. (1996). New technology: Old industrial sociology? *New Technology, Work and Employment, 11*(1), 3–15.

Grimes, S. (1992). Exploiting information and communication technologies for rural development. *Journal of Rural Studies, 8*(3), 269–278.

Haddon, L., & Brynin, M. (2005). The character of telework and the characteristics of teleworkers. *New Technology, Work and Employment, 20*(1), 34–46.

Hupkau, C., & Petrongolo, B. (2020). Work, care and gender during the Covid-19 crisis. *Fiscal Studies, 41*(3), 623–651.

Hjorthol, R. J. (2006). Teleworking in some Norwegian urban areas: Motives and transport effects. *Urban Geography, 27*(7), 610–627.

Hill, E. J., Ferris, M., & Märtinson, V. (2003). Does it matter where you work? A comparison of how three work venues (traditional office, virtual office, and home office) influence aspects of work and personal/family life. *Journal of Vocational Behavior, 63*(2), 220–241.

Howcroft, D., & Rubery, J. (2019). 'Bias in, Bias out': Gender equality and the future of work debate. *Labour & Industry: a journal of the social and economic relations of work, 29*(2), 213–227.

Hynes, M. (2016). Developing (tele) work?: A multi-level sociotechnical perspective of telework in Ireland. *Research in Transportation Economics, 57*, 21–31.

Ishii, K., Nakayama, N., & Yamamoto, I. (2021). Koronaka shoki no Kinkyujitaisengenka niokeru zaitakukinmu no jisshi yoin to Shotoku ya huan ni taisuru eikyo, (Factors for remote work and its impact on income and anxiety in the state of emergency in the spread of Covid-19). *Nihon Rodo Kenkyu Zasshi, 731*, 81–98.

ILO. (2020). *Teleworking during the COVID-19 pandemic and beyond: A practical guide*.

JILPT. (2021). *Results of a survey on the impact of the spread of COVID-19 infection on work and life (JILPT 4th, Interim Report) April 30 2021* (In Japanese).

Kawaguchi, D., & Motegi, H. (2021). Who can work from home? The roles of job tasks and HRM practices. *Journal of Japanese and International Economies, 62*, 101162.

Kawashima, T., Nomura, S., Tanoue, Y., Yoneoka, D., Eguchi, A., Shi, S., & Miyata, H. (2021). The relationship between fever rate and telework implementation as a social distancing measure against the COVID-19 pandemic in Japan. *Public Health, 192*, 12–14.

Kelly, M. M. (1988). The work-at-home revolution. *The Futurist, 22*(6), 28.

Maruyama, T., Hopkinson, P. G., & James, P. W. (2009). A multivariate analysis of work-life balance outcomes from a large-scale telework programme. *New Technology, Work and Employment, 24*(1), 76–88. https://doi.org/10.1111/ntwe.2009.24.issue-1, https://doi.org/10.1111/j.1468-005X.2008.00219.x

Mayo, M., Gomez-Mejia, L., Firfiray, S., Berrone, P., & Villena, V. H. (2016). Leader beliefs and CSR for employees: The case of telework provision. *Leadership & Organization Development Journal, 37*(5), 609–634.

Messenger, J. C., & Gschwind, L. (2016). Three generations of telework: New ICT s and the (R) evolution from home office to virtual office. *New Technology, Work and Employment, 31*(3), 195–208.

Minetake, K. (2020). Terewāku no kōka ni kansuru jisshō kenkyū (Empirical research on the effect of telework). *Journal of Business and Economics, 37*(2), 79–95.

Mokhtarian, P. L. (1991). Defining telecommuting. *Transportation Research Record, 1305*, 273–281.

Nilles, J. (1975). Telecommunications and organizational decentralization. *IEEE Transactions on Communications, 23*(10), 1142–1147.

Nilles, J. M. (1976a). Cities xi: Talk is cheaper: And so may be other forms of telecommuting. *Weighed against the Time, Energy, and Expense of Moving Oneself, IEEE Spectrum, 13*(7), 91–94.

Nilles, J. M. (1976b). *Telecommunications-transportation tradeoff: Options for tomorrow*. John Wiley & Sons Inc.

OECD. (2020). *Supporting people and companies to deal with the COVID-19 virus: Options for an immediate employment and social-policy response.*

Ohtani, A. (2021). Kinkyujitai sengenka ni okeru tomobataraki huhu no kaji ikuji jikan no henka-kodomo wo motu huhu no terewa-ku jokyo wo kouryosite (Change of housekeeping and child care hours between wife and husband under the state of emergency). Works Discussion Paper, No. 50. Recruit Works Institute.

Okubo, T. (2022). Telework in the spread of COVID-19. *Information Economics and Policy, 60*, 100987.

Peters, P., Tijdens, K. G., & Wetzels, C. (2004). Employees' opportunities, preferences, and practices in telecommuting adoption. *Information & Management, 41*(4), 469–482.

Pérez, M. P., Sánchez, A. M., de Luis Carnicer, M. P., & Jiménez, M. J. V. (2004a). The environmental impacts of teleworking. *Management of Environmental Quality, 15*, 656–671.

Pérez, M. P., Sánchez, A. M., de Luis Carnicer, P., & Jiménez, M. J. V. (2004b). A technology acceptance model of innovation adoption: The case of teleworking. *European Journal of Innovation Management, 7*(4), 280–291.

Qvortrup, L. (1989). The nordic telecottages: Community teleservice centres for rural regions. *Telecommunications Policy, 13*(1), 59–68.

Ravalet, E., & Rérat, P. (2019). Teleworking: Decreasing mobility or increasing tolerance of commuting distances? *Built Environment, 45*(4), 582–602.

Rietveld, P. (2011). Telework and the transition to lower energy use in transport: On the relevance of rebound effects. *Environmental Innovation and Societal Transitions, 1*(1), 146–151.

Pérez, M. P., Sánchez, A. M., & de Luis Carnicer, M. P. (2002). Benefits and barriers of telework: Perception differences of human resources managers according to company's operations strategy. *Technovation, 22*(12), 775–783.

Popuri, Y. D., & Bhat, R. R. (2001). On modeling the choice and frequency of home-based telecommuting by individuals. In *83rd annual meeting of the transportation research board* (vol. 1858, No. 1, pp. 55–60).

Sakuragi, T., Tanaka, R., Tsuji, M., Tateishi, S., Hino, A., Ogami, A., Nagata, M., Matsuda, S., & Fujino, Y. (2022). Gender differences in housework and childcare among Japanese workers during the COVID-19 pandemic. *Abstract Journal of Occupational Health, 64*(1). https://doi.org/10.1002/1348-9585.12339

Scott, D. M., Dam, I., Páez, A., & Wilton, R. D. (2012). Investigating the effects of social influence on the choice to telework. *Environment and Planning A, 44*(5), 1016–1031.
Sevilla, A., & Smith, S. (2020). Baby steps: The gender division of childcare during the COVID-19 pandemic. *Oxford Review of Economic Policy, 36*(Supplement_1), S169–S186.
Shin, J. (2021) kolona sigie tellewokeuneun eotteohge bulpyeongdeung-eul jaesaengsanhaneunga?: tellewokeu iyongjaui teugseong mich tellewokeuga nodongsodeug mich jigmu/saenghwal manjogdo-e michin yeonghyang-e daehan tamsaegjeog geomto (How does telework reproduce inequality in times of COVID: An exploratory review of the characteristics of teleworkers and the effect of telework on labor income and job/life satisfaction). In *2021 KLIPS Conference paper*, Korea Labor Institute.
Singer, J. D., & Willett, J. B. (2014). Growth Curve Modeling. In N. Balakrishnan, T. Colton, B. Everitt, W. Piegorsch, F. Ruggeri, & J. L. Teugels (Eds.), *Wiley StatsRef: Statistics reference online.* Wiley.
Son, Y. J. (2022). yuyeongeunmujewa geunlojaui il·saenghwalgyunhyeong - kolona19 ihu jaetaeggeunlo hwagsan-ui yeonghyang-eul jungsim-eulo (The relationship between flexible work arrangements and work-life balance—with a focus on working from home during the COVID-19 pandemic). *26*(2), 37–51.
Stanworth, C. (1998). Telework and the information age. *New Technology, Work and Employment, 13*(1), 51–62.
Sullivan, C. (2003). What's in a name? Definitions and conceptualisations of teleworking and homeworking. *New Technology, Work and Employment, 18*(3), 158–165.
Takahashi, T. (1986). Report on the INS experiment. *Computer Networks and ISDN Systems, 11*(4), 269–276.
Tavares, F., Santos, E., Diogo, A., & Ratten, V. (2020). Teleworking in Portuguese communities during the COVID-19 pandemic. *Journal of Enterprising Communities: People and Places in the Global Economy, 15*, 334–349.
Thulin, E., Vilhelmson, B., & Johansson, M. (2019). New telework, time pressure, and time use control in everyday life. *Sustainability, 11*(11), 3067.
Vilhelmson, B., & Thulin, E. (2016). Who and where are the flexible workers? Exploring the current diffusion of telework in Sweden. *New Technology, Work and Employment, 31*(1), 77–96.
Walls, M., Safirova, E., & Jiang, Y. (2007). What drives telecommuting? Relative impact of worker demographics, employer characteristics, and job types. *Transportation Research Record: Journal of the Transportation Research Board, 2010*(1), 111–120.
Wellman, B., Salaff, J., Dimitrova, D., Garton, L., Gulia, M., & Haythornthwaite, C. (1996). Computer networks as social networks: Collaborative work, telework, and virtual community. *Annual Review of Sociology, 22*(1), 213–238.

Government Reports

Cabinet Office. (2007). Terewāku jinkō baizō akushon puran "Telework population doubling action plan". Retrieved 1 Jan 2023. https://dl.ndl.go.jp/pid/3531345/1/1. Tokyo, Japan.
Cabinet Secretariat. (2021). Chihō sōsei terewāku no suishin ni mukete "Toward the revitalization of local area using telework". Retrieved 1 Jan 2023. https://www.chisou.go.jp/chitele/images/semi09.pdf. Tokyo, Japan.
IT Strategic Headquarters (2010). i-Japan Senryaku 2015 - kokumin shuyaku no 'dejitaru anshin katsuryoku shakai' no jitsugen o mezashite "Towards Digital inclusion & innovation "i-Japan Strategy 2015-Striving to Create a Citizen-Driven, Reassuring & Vibrant Digital Society: Towards Digital inclusion & innovation". https://japan.kantei.go.jp/policy/it/i-JapanStrategy2015_full.pdf, Tokyo, Japan.

IT Strategic Headquarters. (2010). Aratana jōhō tsūshin gijutsu senryaku "A New Strategy in Information and Communications Technology". Retrieved 1 Jan 2023. https://warp.ndl.go.jp/info:ndljp/pid/12187388/japan.kantei.go.jp/policy/it/100511_full.pdf. Tokyo, Japan.
Ministry of Internal Affairs and Communications (MIC). (2021). Heisei 6-nenban tsūshin hakusho "1994 The White paper on communication". Retrieved 1 Jan 2023. https://www.soumu.go.jp/johotsusintokei/whitepaper/h06.html, Tokyo, Japan.
Ministry of Internal Affairs and Communications (MIC) (2021). Tsūshin riyō dōkō chōsa (kigyō-hen) "2021 The communication usage trend survey (Businesses)". Retrieved 1 Jan 2023. https://www.soumu.go.jp/johotsusintokei/statistics/pdf/HR202100002.pdf. Tokyo, Japan.
Ministry of Internal Affairs and Communications (MIC) (2010). Terewāku no dōkō to shōsansei ni kansuru chōsa kenkyū hōkoku-sho "Research Report on Telework Trends and Productivity". Retrieved 1 Jan 2023. https://www.soumu.go.jp/johotsusintokei/linkdata/h22_06_houkoku.pdf. Tokyo, Japan.
Ministry of Land, Infrastructure, Transport and Tourism (MLIT) (2008). THE Telework GUIDEBOOK Kigyō no tame no terewāku dōnyū un'yō gaidobukku "THE Telework GUIDEBOOK: Telework Introduction and Operation Guidebook for Enterprises". Retrieved 1 Jan 2023. https://www.mlit.go.jp/crd/daisei/telework/guidebook/guidebook_gaiyou.pdf. Tokyo, Japan.
Ministry of Land, Infrastructure, Transport and Tourism (MLIT). (2009). 2008-Nendo terewāku jinkō jittai chōsa no kekka ni tsuite "The FY2008 population survey on teleworkers: survey results". Retrieved 1 Jan 2023. http://www.mlit.go.jp/report/press/city03_hh_000002.html. Tokyo, Japan.
Ministry of Land, Infrastructure, Transport and Tourism (MLIT). (2014). Heisei 26-nendo terewāku jinkō jittai chōsa - chōsa kekka no gaiyō "The FY2014 population survey on teleworkers: The summary of survey results". Retrieved 1 Jan 2023. https://www.mlit.go.jp/crd/daisei/telework/docs/26telework_jinko_jittai_gaiyo.pdf. Tokyo, Japan.
Ministry of Land, Infrastructure, Transport and Tourism(MLIT). (2022). Ryō wa 3-nendo terewāku jinkō jittai chōsa — chōsa kekka — "The FY2021 population survey on teleworkers: Survey results". Retrieved 1 Jan 2023. https://www.mlit.go.jp/toshi/daisei/content/001471979.pdf. Tokyo, Japan.
The Japan Institute for labor policy and training (JILPT) (2008). Kigyō no terewāku no jittai ni kansuru chōsa kekka "The results of survey on the state of telework in enterprise". Retrieved 1 Jan 2023. https://www.jil.go.jp/institute/research/2008/documents/050/050.pdf. Tokyo, Japan.
The Japan Institute for labor policy and training (JILPT) (2021). Terewāku: Korona-ka ni okeru sei rōshi no torikumi "Telework: Efforts of government, labour and management in the Covid-19 pandemic".
The Japan Institute for labor policy and training (JILPT). (2022). Shingata koronauirusukansenshō ga kigyō keiei ni oyobosu eikyō ni kansuru chōsa "JILPT panel survey on the impact of COVID-19 on enterprise management". Retrieved 1 Jan 2023. https://www.jil.go.jp/press/documents/20220518b.pdf. Tokyo, Japan.
Tokyo Metropolitan Government (TMG). (2022). Ryō wa 3-nendo tayōna hataraki-kata ni kansuru jittai chōsa (terewāku) kekka hōkoku-sho "The FY2022 Report on the results of the survey on diverse work style (telework)". Retrieved 1 Jan 2023. https://www.hataraku.metro.tokyo.lg.jp/hatarakikata/telework/03report.pdf. Tokyo, Japan.

Chapter 3
Impact of the COVID-19 Pandemic on the Gender Gap in Domestic Labor: Evidence from a Two-Wave Survey in Japan

Junko Nishimura, Jihey Bae, and Kota Toma

Abstract This study explored the gender gap in domestic labor at three time points, namely, before the pandemic (January 2020), during the early stages of the pandemic (May 2020), and more than one year after the expansion (May 2021). Using a two-wave social survey on work and family, this study observed no change in the gender gap in domestic labor for the majority of women and men in the early stages of the pandemic. Alternatively, the study noted a narrowing of the gender gap for 40–50% of the female and male respondents for housework and childcare one year after the outbreak of the pandemic. The associations between time availability, as well as relative resource factors and changes in the gender gap, were more clearly observed in the early stages of the pandemic than one year after the outbreak. Although this study observed a sign of a decline in gender gap for domestic labor one year after the outbreak of the pandemic, it is necessary to exercise caution and qualify such finding. Even in May 2021, a significant difference is still evident between women and men in their frequencies of all the domestic tasks. Furthermore, the data used in this study, which measures women's and men's involvement in housework and childcare based on frequency, may not adequately capture the increased burden of domestic labor on women, which had already been high even before the pandemic.

Keywords Domestic labor · Gender gap · COVID-19

J. Nishimura (✉)
Ochanomizu University, Tokyo, Japan
e-mail: nishimura.junko@ocha.ac.jp

J. Bae
J.F. Oberlin University, Tokyo, Japan
e-mail: jiheybae@obirin.ac.jp

K. Toma
Kyoto University, Kyoto, Japan
e-mail: toma.kota.6t@kyoto-u.ac.jp

S. Matsuda and H. Takenoshita (eds.), *Changes in Work and Family Life in Japan Under COVID-19*, Population Studies of Japan, https://doi.org/10.1007/978-981-99-5850-4_3

3.1 Introduction

In recent years, the gender gap in domestic labor in Japan has demonstrated signs of changes. However, the shifts observed have been modest in size and slow in pace. According to the Survey on Time Use and Leisure Activities, which is conducted every five years, housework time for men with children aged < 6 years has been increasing, and that for women has been decreasing over the past 20 years, which indicates a decline in the gender gap for housework time. However, the housework time of men in 2021 spans 30 min compared with 2 h and 58 min of women (Statistics Bureau of Japan, 2022), which suggests a continued and large gender gap in housework time. Moreover, the gender gap in childcare has remained the same, because the childcare time of not only men but also women has been increasing (Statistics Bureau of Japan, 2022).

The COVID-19 pandemic can be regarded as an event that challenged the conventional division of domestic labor by increasing the demand for domestic work. Increased time at home, which was imposed through the restriction on going out and expansion of working from home, increased frequencies of eating at home due to decreased opportunities to eat out, increased demand for childcare at home due to school closure and difficulty of access to daycare, and increased demand to help children with their studies, led to an increase in domestic labor to be done by family members. In these scenarios, many couples were forced to re-organize the distribution of domestic tasks to address the increased demands.

Two important issues seemingly require examination in terms of the effect of the pandemic on the spousal division of domestic labor. First, whether or not any changes occurred in the gender gap in domestic labor during the pandemic warrants an investigation. The increased demand of domestic labor is assumed to exert opposing effects on the manner in which housework and childcare are divided between wives and husbands. On the one hand, it may promote the sharing of these activities between couples. For example, the proximity between work and home due to working from home can eliminate barriers to housework and childcare, especially for men. Additionally, the increased demand for caregiving for children at home (e.g., due to school closure) may result in spousal collaboration. On the other hand, gender equality may be curtailed. For instance, if one considers the fact that furlough, layoff, and job separation tend to be more common among women (Zhou, 2020), then we can speculate that the COVID-19 pandemic may greatly reduce the bargaining resources of women in marital relationships. This notion could result in the increased burden of domestic labor on women. Meanwhile, men are expected to continue working for long hours; thus, working from home may encourage them to overcommit to work; consequently, this scenario may not necessarily promote the involvement of men in housework and childcare. Furthermore, gender display (Brines, 1994) may work. That is, the conventional division of domestic labor might be maintained, because men who are forced to take furlough attempt to maintain their masculinity.

Second, the gender gap in domestic labor may manifest differently according to the time since the pandemic spread. The pandemic forced changes in lifestyle, particularly during its initial stages (from April to May 2020, under the first state of emergency in Japan). Specifically, these lifestyle changes include staying home, refraining from eating out, working from home, and online learning at home for children. A few of these lifestyle changes have returned to pre-pandemic conditions, but others have remained altered and persistent. In Japan, for example, schools (for children aged 6–18 years) were closed from February 28 to May 2020, but no nationwide school closures occurred thereafter.[1] Alternatively, the implementation rate for telework among companies increased from March to May 2020 and remained higher in March 2021 compared with pre-pandemic rates (Ministry of Internal Affairs and Communications, 2021). This observation indicates that certain companies have continued to implement telework after the pandemic. Thus, the gender gap in domestic labor may display different features due to the time lapse since the outbreak of the pandemic and the associated changes in lifestyle.

Therefore, this study aims to examine the impact of the pandemic on gender gap in domestic labor in Japan. Based on previous studies on the gender division of domestic labor, the current study examines how time availability factors and the relative resources between wives and husbands are associated with changes in the gender gap in domestic labor during the pandemic through analyses of survey data. Furthermore, this study, although partially using retrospective data, explores the gender gap in domestic labor between couples at three time points, namely, before the pandemic (January 2020), during the early stages of the pandemic (May 2020), and more than one year after the expansion of the pandemic (May 2021). Doing so will enable the study to distinguish between changes that occurred during the early stages of the pandemic and those over a longer period of time. In this manner, we can examine whether or not the pandemic caused only a temporary shift or a more long-term consequence in the gender gap in domestic labor in Japan.

We briefly review the Japanese context of the COVID-19 pandemic and the measures taken by the government. After the first case of infection was confirmed in January 2020, COVID-19 spread throughout the country, and the first state of emergency was declared in April–May 2020. A state of emergency was then declared for a total of three times, namely, January 2021, April 2021, and July 2021; however, the details requested by the Japanese government for behavioral restrictions differed for each instance. Although the declaration of a state of emergency in Japan was considered a soft lockdown (Kuroda, 2020), and although the requests of the government for people to restrict their behaviors were less severe compared with those of other countries, the first emergency declaration was the most extensive one and strongly requested people to restrict their behaviors. For example, the Japanese government asked a wide range of industries, including restaurants, department stores, and movie

[1] The Ministry of Education, Culture, Sports, Science and Technology (MEXT) announced that until December 2020, schools were temporarily closed after confirming positive cases of COVID-19 in schools. The closure was in effect according to the number of days necessary for local public health centers to test and identify people in close contact with COVID-19. After December 2020, the MEXT asked the schools to decide whether or not to close based on the status of the pandemic in the region and the opinion of the local public health centers, even when positive cases of COVID-19 were confirmed in schools.

theaters, to reduce their operating hours or close their stores. It also urged people to postpone or cancel events involving large numbers of participants. In addition, schools were closed nationwide only under the first emergency declaration. Therefore, the early stage of the pandemic (May 2020), which is one of the foci of this paper, was the period in which the Japanese government requested the most stringent restriction of behaviors from its citizens as part of its measures against the pandemic to date.

The remainder of this study is structured as follows. Section 3.2 provides an overview of the research framework for the division of domestic labor and related empirical findings from previous studies. Section 3.3 conducts a review on recent research on the changes in gender gap in relation to domestic labor during the pandemic. Section 3.4 identifies possible factors that influence these changes and draw the hypotheses. Section 3.5 describes the data and analytical procedures. Section 3.6 presents the results of the descriptive analysis regarding changes in the frequencies of housework and childcare by the respondents and their spouses. It also presents the results of the multinomial logit models of changes in the gender gap between January and May 2020 and between January 2020 and May 2021. Finally, Sect. 3.7 discusses a potential shift in gender gap in relation to domestic labor during the pandemic and future directions for changes in gender inequality in the Japanese society.

3.2 Previous Research on the Division of Domestic Labor

Housework and childcare have been regarded as closely related activities, although the factors that determine the extent of sharing between spouses may differ for both activities (Ishi-Kuntz & Coltrane, 1992). Accordingly, general middle-range theories have been used to explain the gendered allocation of housework and childcare: time availability, relative resources, and ideology (Kamo, 1988; Shelton & John, 1996).

The explanation of time availability assumes that couples aim to meet the demand for domestic labor through gender-neutral strategies for labor allocation. Couples are assumed to meet the demands for household labor by assigning tasks to the person with more time availability, which is typically measured by the number of work hours or employment status. The explanation of relative resources focuses on the relative resources of each spouse such as earnings and level of education. Assuming that domestic labor is an undesirable activity for both spouses, the person with more resources is regarded as holding more bargaining power and, therefore, does less domestic work. Finally, the explanation of ideology focuses on individual preferences in domestic tasks, which is often measured by the attitudes of individuals toward the gender division of labor. This explanation assumes that women and men with more egalitarian attitudes toward family roles will share domestic labor more equally.

Previous studies in the Japanese context provided support for time availability. Specifically, scholars suggested that the shorter work hours of men are a driving force in their involvement in domestic labor (Matsuda, 2000; Sasaki, 2018). Meanwhile, other scholars reported mixed findings on relative resources. The effect of relative resources on the performance of husbands in domestic tasks seemingly differed according to the measurement of relative resources or on whether or not the studies examine housework or childcare (Bae, 2009; Matsuda, 2006). Furthermore, a few studies indicated that the effect of spousal relative earnings on the performance of husbands in domestic labor is curvilinear (Ando, 2012). This finding suggested gender display, that is, economically dependent husbands dogender by doing less housework (Brines, 1994). Moreover, other studies in Japan suggested that the gender ideology of spouses is not significantly related to the sharing of domestic tasks. Using nationally representative samples, Matsuda (2006) found no significant association between men's gender ideology and their frequencies of housework and childcare.

The current study examines how the existing frameworks of the division of domestic labor may explain changes in the allocation of such tasks during the COVID-19 pandemic in Japan. As the data do not contain measures of gender ideology, the discussion focuses on time availability and relative resources.

3.3 The COVID-19 Pandemic and the Gender Gap in Domestic Labor

As previously mentioned, changes in work and family life due to the COVID-19 pandemic may exert two opposing effects on marital equality in domestic labor. On the one hand, various measures taken to prevent the spread of infection (e.g., working from home and refraining from going out) may have promoted equality in domestic labor mainly by increasing men's participation in housework and childcare. On the other hand, the increased precariousness of the employment of women during the pandemic may have forced couples to return to the gendered division of labor, which, thus, deepened the previously existing gender inequality.

Previous studies on marital equality in domestic labor during the pandemic suggested two possibilities. First, a few studies demonstrated that the increase in the domestic labor of men has reduced gender gap mainly in western societies (Carlson et al., 2021; Craig & Churchill, 2021; Hupkau & Petrongolo, 2020; Shafer et al., 2020). For example, Shafer et al. (2020) analyzed the division of domestic labor among couples in Canada during the initial period of the pandemic in 2020. The authors concluded that the gendered division of domestic labor is shifting toward equality, because a significant number of fathers have increased their share of housework. In a related study in the United States, Carlson et al. (2021) argued that although mothers have increased their responsibilities at home, fathers have also increased their contribution, which resulted in more equal share in domestic labor.

Moreover, various studies pointed out that the changes in gender gap differed according to the type of domestic task. For example, Craig and Churchill (2021) found that equality has increased for childcare but not for housework in Australia.

Meanwhile, according to Hupkau and Petrongolo (2020), the gender gap in housework has narrowed in the United Kingdom, whereas the gender gap in childcare has widened. The authors also argued that gender roles became increasingly ambiguous in many British households during the pandemic, because a certain number of men have assumed the role of a primary caregiver. These studies supported the expectation that marital equality in domestic labor will increase during the pandemic, although scholars observed different trends for various types of domestic work.

Second, studies reported that the gap in domestic labor worsened or, at least, was maintained during the pandemic. For instance, Sevilla and Smith (2020) conducted a study on British parents with children aged <12 years and proposed that mothers carried the majority of the burden associated with childcare. Furthermore, the additional hours of childcare performed by women were less sensitive to their employment than they were for men. In related studies, Chin et al. (2020) and Kim and Choi (2021) examined changes due to the pandemic in family life in Korea and argued that women were more likely than men to report an increase in housework during the initial days (Chin et al., 2020) and half a year (Kim & Choi, 2021) following the spread of COVID-19. Similarly, Dunatchik et al. (2021) conducted a study on parents in the United States and reported little evidence that the gender gap in domestic labor declined during the early phase of the pandemic (April, 2020) compared with before the pandemic. The authors argued that although men became more involved in housework and childcare, gender division in domestic work remained the same, because women also increased their involvement. Furthermore, Del Boca et al. (2022) conducted surveys during two waves of COVID-19 (April and November 2020) in Italy. The authors found that the gender gap in domestic labor was widest during the first wave of the pandemic. Furthermore, although it was less pronounced during the second wave, it remained higher than that before COVID-19.

In Japan, some studies suggested that women carried much of the additional burden of domestic labor during the early days of COVID-19, at a time when the first state of emergency was declared from April to May 2020. For example, Ochiai and Suzuki (2020) conducted a survey in April 2020 on individuals who worked from home (themselves or their family members). The results indicated that 36% of women with children expressed difficulty with housework and childcare compared with 15% of men with children and only 10% of women without children. Although this survey was limited to individuals working from home, the finding suggests that the increased burden of domestic work during the so-called stay-at-home period in Japan may have been mainly allocated to women with children. In addition, Yokomaku (2020) reported that although the shares of housework and childcare for women declined and that the shares for men increased during January 2020 (pre-pandemic) and April 2020, the amount of domestic labor conducted by women nevertheless increased due to the additional demand for care work. These studies supported the expectation that the pandemic will increase the burden of domestic work on women, quantitatively and qualitatively, and that the existing gender gap will increase.

On the other hand, there are some studies suggesting the decline in the gender gap, particularly in the studies that examined the gender gap in domestic work up to August 2020, a little more than six months after the outbreak of the pandemic. For example,

Ishibashi et al. (2021) conducted a survey in August 2020, and retrospectively asked the time use of their respondents in the period before the pandemic and during the first declaration of emergency (from April to May 2020), as well as their time use at the time of survey. They found that while women's housework time increased during April and May 2020, and returned to the same level as before the pandemic in August 2020, men's housework time increased during April and May 2020, and did not decrease to the pre-pandemic level in August 2020. Additionally, Hirai and Watanabe (2021) reported that the number of men who assumed the role of primary caregiver increased in April–May 2020, and the number of such men in August 2020 was still greater than that of pre-pandemic period. These studies suggest that some lifestyle changes triggered by the pandemic might have reduced the gender gap in domestic labor in Japan.

3.4 Factors Associated with Changes in the Gender Gap in Domestic Labor During the Pandemic

How could the existing frameworks of the division of domestic labor explain these changes in the allocation of domestic tasks during the pandemic? This section presents a review of the previous research in terms of the factors that led to changes in the gender gap in domestic labor during the pandemic. This study mainly focuses on time availability and relative resources and then draws its hypotheses.

According to Shafer et al. (2020), the increased sharing of household chores and equalization of domestic labor in Canada was consistently observed among fathers working from home. In Italy and the United States, similar results were reported in which an increase in time at home among men due to work from home, reduced work hours, or unemployment led to an increase in domestic work of fathers (Carlson et al., 2021; Del Boca et al., 2022; Dunatchik et al., 2021). Sevilla and Smith (2020) also found that although mothers continued to carry the majority of the tasks associated with childcare, households whose men did not work illustrated signs of the sharing of childcare in a more equal manner. These findings suggest that changes in the work practices of men that occurred during the pandemic, such as working from home and furlough, may have eliminated the structural constraints that previously prevented them from sharing domestic labor. Specifically, working from home created added time for participation in domestic work by reducing commute time and increasing flexibility in the use of time during the day. In other words, working from home will encourage men, whose time availability for performing domestic labor was previously constrained due to long working and commuting hours, to do more domestic work. Accordingly, this scenario promoted the equal allocation of domestic labor between couples.

On the contrary, studies suggested that working from home for women and men did not influence or even worsened the gender gap in domestic work. Men increased their contribution to domestic work when working from home, but the gender gap in domestic labor remained the same, because women increased their contribution more than men did (Dunatchik et al., 2021; Lyttelton et al., 2021). In addition, Lyttelton et al. (2021) illustrated that although the gender gap in childcare is smaller for women and men working from home than those working on-site, the gender gap in housework is larger for those working from home. The authors argued that the reason is that men are less responsive to the onerous aspects of housekeeping needs compared with those of childcare needs, which is more enjoyable and meaningful.

Being on furlough, on the one hand, increases time availability and potentially promotes the equal allocation of domestic labor. On the other hand, furlough particularly for men can threaten their breadwinner role, which can lead to a gender display, that is, men's reduced (or women's increased) domestic labor, which results in the maintenance or even the widening of the existing gender gap. Therefore, we put forward the following hypotheses:

Hypothesis 1: The gender gap in housework and childcare became more/less equal when husbands worked from home during the COVID-19 pandemic.

Hypothesis 2: The gender gap in housework and childcare became more/less equal when husbands were furloughed during the COVID-19 pandemic.

In terms of relative resources, which is one of the existing frameworks for explaining the division of domestic labor, the increase in domestic labor during the pandemic may be allocated more to the person with less bargaining power, that is, those with less resources in their hands. According to Shafer et al. (2020), an increase in the domestic work hours of men is dependent on the employment status and income of their wives. In other words, husbands were more likely to take care of the children if their wives earned more income, and the participation of husbands in childcare was less likely to increase when they were the primary breadwinners. Similarly, Carlson et al. (2021) examined changes in the division of domestic labor between couples and found that they were associated with relative income. Specifically, when the husbands were the sole/main breadwinners, they did not share domestic labor, and the wives were responsible for the majority of the burden. Conversely, when the wives were the sole/primary breadwinners, the husbands were more likely to share housework and childcare. These findings suggested that the explanation for relative resources is supported to explain the changes in gender gap in domestic labor during the pandemic. The explanation stated that individuals who possess more resources, such as education and earning, will hold more bargaining power to avoid domestic work. Therefore, we present the following hypothesis.

Hypothesis 3: During the pandemic, spouses with relatively high levels of education and earnings were more likely to change the division of domestic labor in a manner that is advantageous to them.

3.5 Methods

3.5.1 Data and Samples

This study used data from the first and second waves of the Survey on Work and Life under COVID-19 (WLCV).[2] This study analyzed the data of individuals who responded to the first and second waves of the surveys. After excluding cases with missing values in the variables, the study included a total of 411 cases (female: 252; male: 159). For the analysis of childcare, only cases in which the youngest child was aged ≤8 years were included, which resulted in 185 and 115 cases for women and men, respectively.

The data are not a matched dataset with responses from both spouses. A previous study that examined housework by wives and husbands on the basis of matched data found discrepancies in inter-spouse responses, particularly those with regard to the performance of husbands in housework (Kamo, 2000). The current study considers the existence of such bias in the responses of the participants due to the perspectives of the wives and husbands. Therefore, the study separately analyzed the responses of the women and men. Notably, for female respondents, the responses for wives refer to themselves, whereas wives refer to their spouses for male respondents.

3.5.2 Measures

3.5.2.1 Frequency and Changes in Housework and Childcare

The study constructed three variables to examine the frequencies of housework and childcare, namely, the frequency of housework and childcare for the respondent and spouse in January 2020, May 2020, and May 2021; the change in the frequencies of housework and childcare for the respondent and spouse between time points; and the change in spousal gender gap of housework and childcare between the time points. Out of the three, the third variable was used as the dependent variable in the multinomial logit model.

The survey asked the respondents about the frequencies of housework and childcare for themselves and their spouses in January 2020, May 2020, and May 2021. The first survey was conducted in November 2020; thus, the respondents were requested to retrospectively answer about such frequency in January and May 2020. Specifically, the respondents were asked about preparing meals and doing dishes in five categories, namely, 20 times a week or more; 14–19 times per week; 7–13 times per week; 1–6 times per week; and less than once per week. The respondents were also asked about shopping for groceries, doing laundry, cleaning, playing with children, and personal care for children across five categories: 1 = nearly every day (6–7 times

[2] See Chap. 2 for details on the WLCV survey.

per week), 2 = 4–5 times per week, 3 = 2–3 times per week, 4 = approximately once per week, and 5 = hardly ever.

Using the aforementioned items, the study scored the frequency of housework and childcare for the respondents and their spouses for each time point. Meal preparation and doing dishes were scored as follows: 21 for 20 or more times per week; 16.5 for 14–19 times per week; 10 for 7–13 times per week; 3.5 for 1–6 times per week; and 0 for less than once per week. Additionally, shopping for groceries, doing laundry, cleaning, playing with children, and personal care for children were scored as follows: 6.5 for almost every day; 4.5 for 4–5 times per week; 2.5 for 2–3 times per week; 1 for approximately once per week; and 0 for hardly ever.

Regarding changes in the frequencies of housework and childcare between the time points for the respondents and their spouses, the study formulated variables for meal (e.g., preparing meals and doing the dishes) and childcare (e.g., playing with children and personal care for children). We focused on these items, because these household chores and childcare are not deferrable, and the pandemic has seemingly increased the demand for these aspects within families. The specific procedure for creating the variables was as follows. We calculated the (1) total scores for preparing meals and doing the dishes, playing with children and personal care for children, respectively. (2) For meal and childcare, we took the difference between time points about the respondents and their spouses. (3) If the difference calculated in (2) was 0, >0, or <0, then it was categorized as no change, increased, or decreased, respectively.

Finally, changes in spousal gender gap for meal and childcare were created as follows. We calculated (1) the differences between the respondents and their spouses for meal and childcare at each time point. Positive values indicate that wives do more housework or childcare than do their husbands. We then calculated for (2) the difference between time points for the values in (1). (3) If the difference was 0, >0, and <0, then it was categorized as no change, increased, decreased, respectively.

3.5.2.2 Independent and Control Variables

Time availability and relative resources were set as the independent variables. For time availability, we used measures of the experiences of the husbands of working from home, the experiences of the respondents of being furloughed, employment status of the female respondents, and number of weekly work hours of the male respondents. For changes in gender gap in domestic labor during the early stage of the pandemic (from January to May 2020), the experiences of the husbands of working from home in May 2020, the experiences of the respondents of being furloughed between January and November 2020, the employment status of the female respondents, and work hour of the male respondents per week in May 2020 were used. In the analyses of the gender gap on one year after the outbreak of the pandemic (from January 2020 to May 2021), we considered husbands working from home in May 2021, the employment status of the female respondents and weekly work hours of the male respondents in May 2021. We excluded the experiences of the respondents of being furloughed, because less than 10% of the respondents were furloughed in

2021, which will be presented in the following descriptive statistics. For the measure of working from home, a dummy variable takes a value of 1 if the respondents worked from home for at least one day in May 2020 (or in May 2021); otherwise, it takes a value of 0. Individuals who were not employed were coded as 0. We only consider husbands working from home, because, a relatively small number of wives worked from home at the time, as will be presented in the descriptive statistics.

For the variable of being furloughed, the term "furlough" refers to *kyugyo* in Japanese. It is not a permanent layoff or dismissal but a temporary suspension from work while maintaining one's employment contract with an employer. The questionnaire for the first wave asked, "Have you experienced being furloughed since January of this year?" Notably, a possibility exists that a few furloughs occurred after May 2020 (until November 2020, at the time of the first survey) in the analysis of the gender gap from January to May 2020; but we cannot specify their timings in the data. A dummy variable for the experience of being furloughed was coded as 1 if the respondents were furloughed; otherwise, they were coded as 0.[3] Individuals who were not employed were coded as 0.

We created three categories for the employment status of women, namely, regular employment, nonregular employment or self-employed, and not employed. As only 8 (3.2%) and 11 (4.4%) women were self-employed in May 2020 and May 2021, respectively, they were classified under the nonregular employment category. In terms of the work hours of the husbands, we used those in May 2020 and May 2021.

For relative resources, we considered the relative resources of the couples in education and earnings. With regard to education, we created three categories that combined the educational backgrounds of the respondents and their spouses, namely, (1) wives and husbands have the same levels of education, (2) wives have college level education and husbands have less than high school level education, and (3) wives have less than high school level education and husbands have college level education. The same level category includes couples in which both spouses achieved less than high school education and both spouses achieved a college level education. Although these two groups differ in their characteristics, we integrated them into one category to capture relative resources. The educational background of the respondents and their spouses were asked only at the first wave of the survey; therefore, the same values are used for the analyses of the early stages of the pandemic and up to one year later. Then, relative resources in earnings were measured using the ratio of the annual earnings of the wives to their husbands. Each wave of the survey asked about the annual earnings of the respondents and their spouses in the previous year. This aspect enabled the examination of the relationship between spousal relative earnings prior to the analyzed time points and subsequent changes in the gender gap in domestic labor. We set three categories for the earnings ratio of the wives, namely, <20%, 20–50%, and >50%.

[3] In total, 21% of women and 18% of men experienced being furloughed between January and November 2020. Among those who experienced being furloughed, 63% of women were under nonregular employment, and 78% of men were under regular employment in May 2020. The average lengths of furlough was 37 and 19 days for women and men, respectively, and 60 and 72% of women and men, respectively, received allowances during the furlough.

For the control variables, we used the number of children, a dummy variable for the youngest child aged <6 years, and the frequencies of meal of the respondents and spouses in January 2020. The number of children and the frequencies of childcare for both spouses in January 2020 were used for the analyses of childcare. Frequencies of meal and childcare by the respondents and their spouses in January 2020 were retrospectively asked at the first wave of the survey.

3.5.3 *Analytical Procedures*

The following procedures were used for analysis. First, we examined the frequencies of housework and childcare by time point and gender. Next, we investigated changes in the frequencies of housework and childcare using the meal and childcare variables. We also focused on changes in the spousal gender gap for meal and childcare between the time points. We then applied multinomial logit models with the changes in the gender gap for meal and childcare between January and May 2020 and between January 2020 and May 2021 as the dependent variables. The reference category for the dependent variables was no change, while we examined the effects of the independent variables on the increased and decreased in gender gap.

3.6 Results

3.6.1 *Descriptive Statistics*

Table 3.1 presents the descriptive statistics of the variables in the multivariate analyses. The data collected from the first wave of survey are listed under the May 2020 column, and those obtained from the second wave of survey are listed under the May 2021 column. Although the variables of being furloughed during January–May 2021 and wives working from home in May 2020 and 2021 were not used in the multivariate analyses, these figures are included in the table, because they were deemed helpful in understanding the changes in the manner that people worked during the pandemic. In addition, Table 3.1 presents the mean values of meal and childcare for women and men (and their spouses) in January 2020, May 2020, and May 2021.

As shown in Table 3.1, approximately 20% of the women and men were furloughed during the early stage of the pandemic. These figures decreased to approximately 10% until one year later. Although >10% of wives were working from home in May 2020, <10% of wives were doing so in May 2021. Furthermore, this result indicated that significant gender gaps existed in meal and childcare before the onset of the pandemic (January 2020). For example, wives do meal-related housework five to seven times more frequently than their husbands do, although certain differences were observed in women's and men's answers. The frequencies of meal and childcare

Table 3.1 Descriptive statistics

	Women ($n = 252$)				Men ($n = 159$)			
	May 2020		May 2021		May 2020		May 2021	
	Mean	Sd	Mean	Sd	Mean	Sd	Mean	Sd
Respondents furloughed[a]	0.21		0.10		0.18		0.09	
Wives working from home	0.13		0.08		0.11		0.08	
Husbands working from home	0.25		0.13		0.28		0.13	
Wives' employment status								
Regular emplolyment	0.21		0.23					
Nonregular employment, or self-employed	0.45		0.52					
Not employed	0.35		0.25					
Husbands' weekly work hour					43.33	12.59	44.27	12.30
Education[b]								
Both partners less than high school, or both partners college	0.69				0.64			
Wife college, husband less than high school	0.15				0.20			
Husband college, wife less than high school	0.16				0.17			
Wives' earnings ratio								
Less than 20%	0.58		0.61		0.57		0.58	
20–50%	0.21		0.18		0.18		0.20	
More than 50%	0.21		0.21		0.25		0.23	
Number of children	2.20	0.76	2.23	0.77	2.09	0.76	2.11	0.75
Youngest child 6 years or younger	0.61		0.58		0.63		0.64	
Frequencies of wives' "meal" in Jan. 2020	35.12	8.23			34.27	9.78		

(continued)

Table 3.1 (continued)

	Women ($n = 252$)				Men ($n = 159$)			
	May 2020		May 2021		May 2020		May 2021	
	Mean	Sd	Mean	Sd	Mean	Sd	Mean	Sd
Frequencies of husbands' "meal" in Jan. 2020	5.24	7.42			7.62	9.03		
Frequencies of wives' "meal"	36.41	8.16	34.70	7.94	34.95	9.27	33.49	9.36
Frequencies of husbands' "meal"	6.00	8.02	6.41	8.13	8.25	9.56	9.36	9.11
	Women ($n = 185$)				Men ($n = 115$)			
Frequencies of wives' "childcare" in Jan. 2020	11.76	1.95			11.37	2.21		
Frequencies of husbands' "childcare" in Jan. 2020	5.01	3.94			7.35	4.32		
Frequencies of wives' "childcare"	12.21	1.63	11.54	2.05	11.51	2.20	11.08	2.50
Frequencies of husbands' "childcare"	5.42	3.95	5.61	3.90	7.74	4.27	7.54	4.33

Notes [a] For "May 2020," the percentages of respondents being furloughed during January and November 2020 are shown. The value for "May 2021" represents the proportion of respondents being furloughed during January and May 2021
[b] The educational backgrounds of the respondents and their spouses are asked only at the first wave of the survey; therefore, the same values are used for the analyses of the early stages of the pandemic and up to one year later

of the wives seemingly increased from January to May 2020, then decreased from May 2020 to January 2021. Alternatively, the frequencies of the husbands for both variables also seemingly increased from January 2020 to May 2021, although only modestly. We will examine these points in detail in the followings.

Figure 3.1 presents the mean scores of the frequencies of housework and childcare of the respondents for three time points, namely, January 2020, May 2020, and May 2021. The score for each item for housework and childcare was calculated according to the procedure described in Sect. 5.2.1. The figures reveal that the scores of the women are higher than those of the men for all items for housework and childcare and for all time points. This finding suggests that it is hardly possible to conclude that the gender gap in domestic labor has substantially narrowed over one year after the outbreak of the pandemic.

With regard to the differences in the frequencies of housework between time points, the frequencies for women for meal preparation and doing dishes increased from January 2020 to May 2020, then decreased from May 2020 to May 2021. Conversely, the frequencies of the men for meal preparation and doing dishes displayed gradual increase during the one-year period from January 2020 to May 2021. The frequencies of women for shopping for groceries decreased from January 2020 to May 2020, then increased from May 2020 to May 2021, whereas the men did not exhibit much change between time points. Moreover, the change in doing laundry between time points for women and men is minimal, while only the men

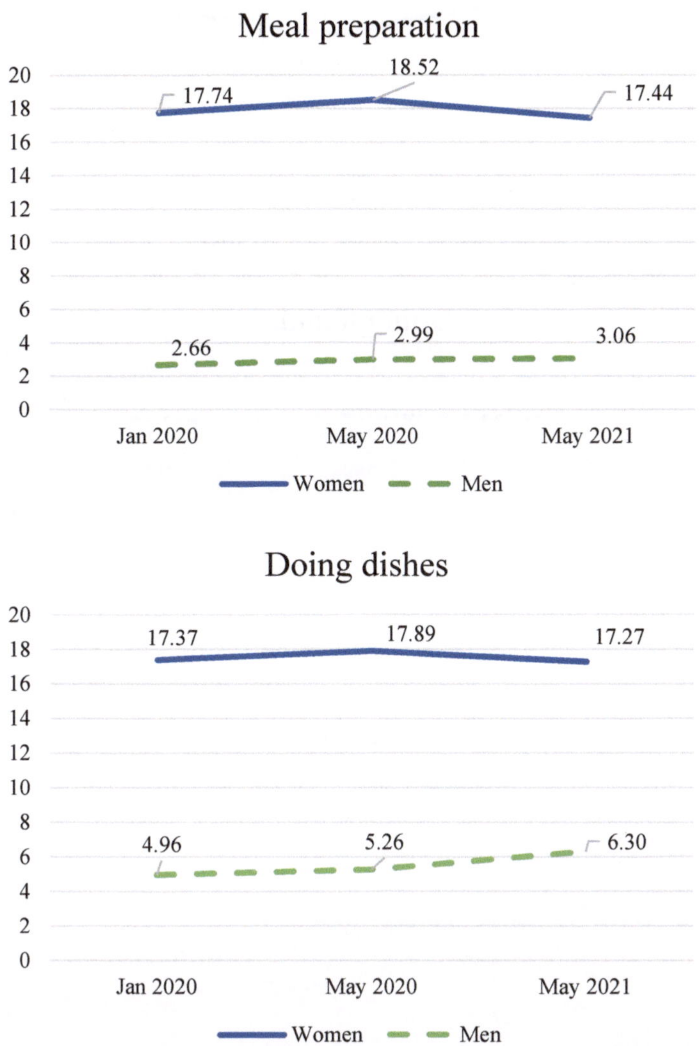

Fig. 3.1 Frequencies of housework and childcare in January 2020, May 2020, and May 2021

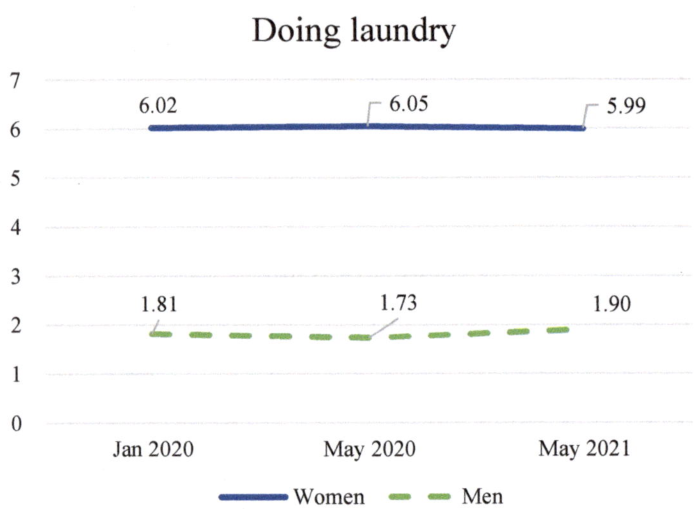

Fig. 3.1 (continued)

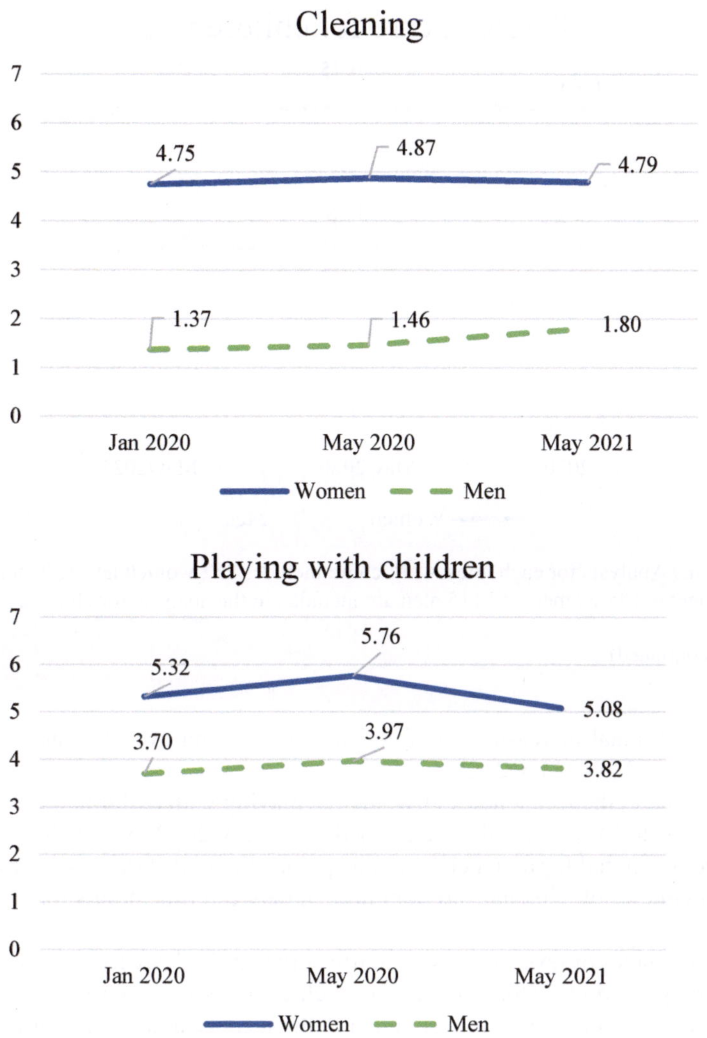

Fig. 3.1 (continued)

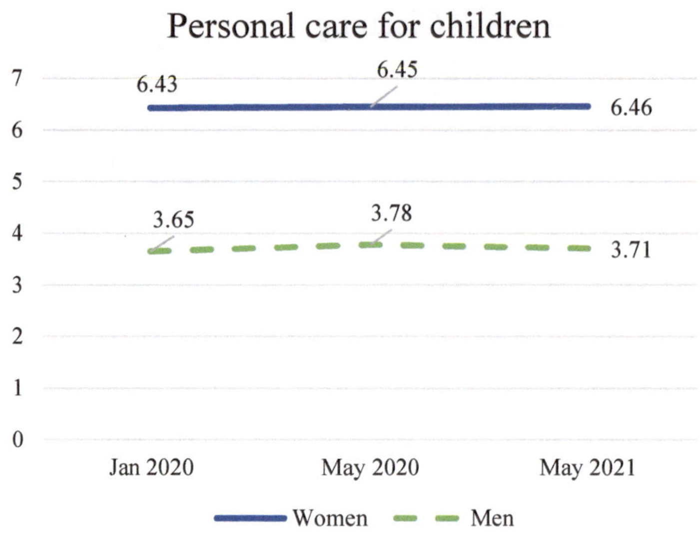

Notes Analysis for each housework chore includes 252 women and 159 men, whereas 185 women and 115 men are included in the analysis for childcare.

Fig. 3.1 (continued)

displayed a gradual increase in the frequency of cleaning over the one-year period from January 2020 to May 2021.

For childcare, the frequencies of women in playing with children increased from January 2020 to May 2020, then decreased from May 2020 to May 2021, whereas no change was noted for men between time points. Small differences were observed in the frequencies of personal care for children between time points for women and men.

The frequencies of several items for housework and childcare for women increased from January to May 2020. For men, no such changes were observed. This result suggests that women, not men, responded to the increased demands for housework and childcare due to emergent responses in the early stages of the pandemic, such as the restriction on going out and school closure in May 2020. Eventually, as people began to coexist with the pandemic and return to their daily routines, the frequencies of housework and childcare for women returned to pre-pandemic levels. The only exception is frequency of shopping, which declined from January to May 2020, because people were requested to refrain from going out under the state of emergency declared in April 2020. This frequency increased from May 2020 to May 2021 but did not return to pre-pandemic levels. This finding may suggest that over the course of the pandemic, a few of the shopping behavior of women were replaced by alternative means such as online shopping.

The frequencies of housework and childcare for men exhibited a trend that differed from those of women. Although the frequencies of the men for many household chores remained the same between time points, their frequencies of doing dishes and cleaning slowly increased over the one-year period following the pandemic. This result suggests that the involvement of men in domestic work has increased, albeit modestly.

We then focus on the frequencies of meal (the sum of the frequencies of meal preparation and doing dishes) and childcare (the sum of the frequencies of playing with children and personal care for children) and examine the changes in their frequencies based on responses for each time point. Meal and childcare were created according to the procedure described in Sect. 5.2.1.

Figure 3.2 indicates that the overwhelming majority (80–90%) of women and men indicated no change in the frequencies of meal and childcare between January and May 2020. Although a relatively high percentage of the responses of the women to meal changed, approximately 80% of them revealed no change.

Examining the figure regarding changes from May 2020 to May 2021, more women and men seemingly experienced changes during this period compared with the early stages of the pandemic. More women displayed decreased, instead of increased, frequencies of meal and childcare. This finding may be related to the fact that during this period, people were returning to their daily routines while coexisting with the pandemic. Alternatively, while a few men displayed increased frequencies of meal and childcare, others decreased. This result suggests that men began to alter their involvement in domestic work after approximately six months since the outbreak of the pandemic.

Furthermore, the results regarding changes from January 2020 to May 2021 indicate that nearly 50% of the women experienced changes in the frequencies of meal after more than one year since the pandemic, with slightly more women decreasing (27%) than increasing (21%) their frequencies. Nearly 60% of the men changed their frequencies of meal with more men increasing (36%) than decreasing (21%) their involvement. With regard to childcare, the frequencies of nearly 70% of the women remained the same. Alternatively, more than 60% of the men exhibited a change with more men increasing (35%) than decreasing (29%) their frequencies. Among the women and men who experienced changes in meal and childcare, more men experienced an increase than a decrease, whereas more women experienced a decrease than an increase. This finding implied a certain level of narrowing of the gender gap in domestic labor.

To further examine whether or not the respondents experienced changes in spousal gender gap in domestic work, Fig. 3.3 presents changes in the gender gap in meal and childcare between the respondents and their spouses across the time points. The measures for spousal gender gap in meal and childcare were generated according to the procedures described in Sect. 5.2.1. The figure on the upper panel indicates no change in the gender gaps for both variables for the majority of the couples from January 2020 to May 2020. In addition, it also indicated that more female respondents experienced an increase in the gender gap in meal than did male respondents. Alternatively, the figures for the periods between May 2020 and May 2021 and between January 2020 and May 2021, which are displayed at the middle and bottom panels, indicated that the majority of the respondents experienced changes in the gender gap

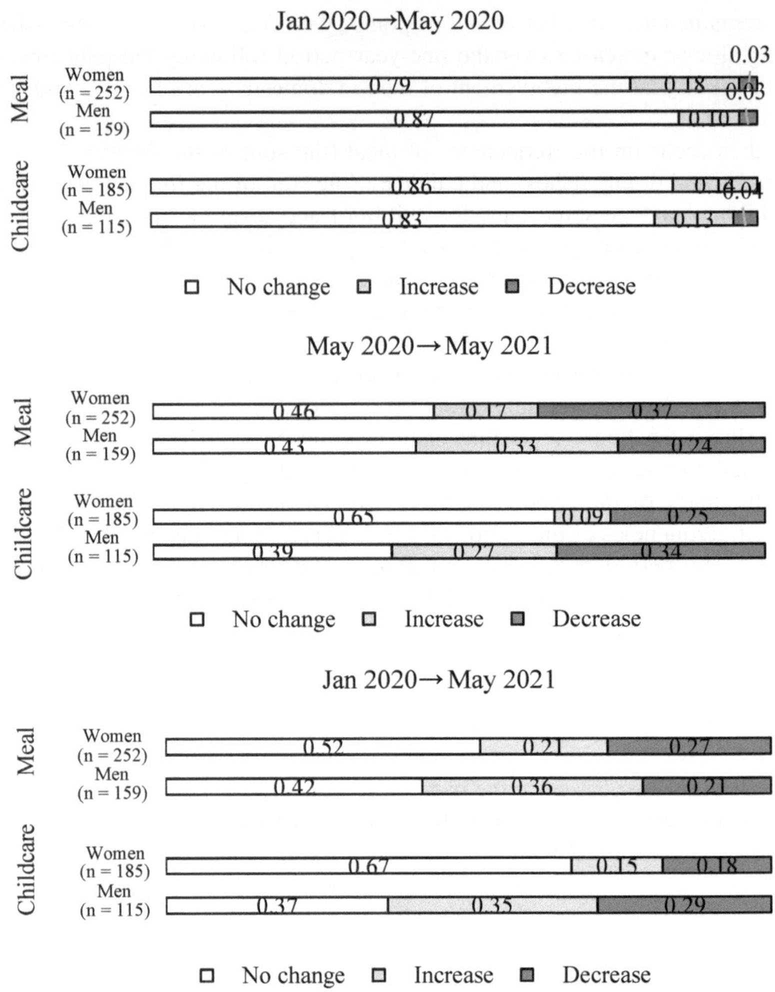

Notes Some of the totals do not add up to 100% (1.0) due to rounding.

Fig. 3.2 Changes in frequencies of housework and childcare between time points

for meal and childcare. More respondents experienced a decrease in gender gap than those who experienced an increase for women and men.

Therefore, although it is impossible to conclude that the gender gap in domestic labor has diminished, given the fact that a significant gap exists in the frequencies of all domestic tasks between women and men (Fig. 3.1) even one year after the outbreak of the pandemic, a possibility exists that the pandemic triggered a slow and gradual change in lifestyles (e.g., men becoming more aware of the need for domestic labor as they spent more time at home), which led to behavioral changes in women and men regarding domestic labor.

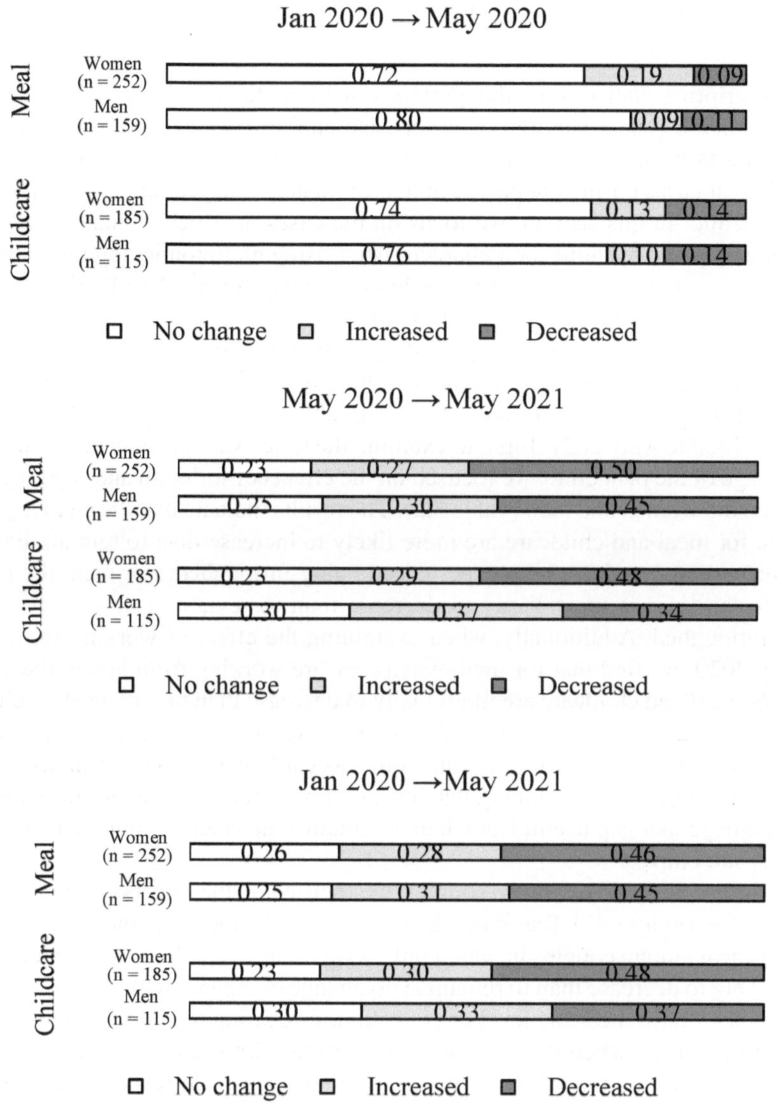

Notes A few of the totals do not add up to 100% (1.0) due to rounding.

Fig. 3.3 Changes in spousal gender gap in housework and childcare between time points

In the multivariate analyses in the next section, we examine which lifestyle changes and characteristics of the respondents are associated with the changes in the gender gap in domestic labor in the early stages of the pandemic as well as one year after the outbreak.

3.6.2 Multivariate Analysis

The descriptive statistics in the previous section demonstrated that no change occurred in the gender gap for housework and childcare in the majority of the cases during the early stage of the pandemic. Meanwhile, shifts in gender gap occurred in a number of cases during the period of approximately one year after the outbreak of the pandemic. In this section, we focus on the cases in which a change was noted in gender gap and examine their characteristics using multinomial logit models. The dependent variables were the changes in gender gap for meal and childcare from January to May 2020 and from January 2020 and May 2021. The responses of the women and men were examined separately in the following analyses.

Tables 3.2 and 3.3 present the results of the analysis.[4] Table 3.2 indicates changes in gender gap during January and May 2020, and Table 3.3 displays changes from January 2020 to May 2021. First, to examine the time availability factors during the early stage of the pandemic, we focused on the effects of furlough and working from home on the women and men (Table 3.2). The results indicate that the gender gap for women for meal and childcare are more likely to increase than to remain the same (no change) among those who experienced being furloughed. For men, the gender gap for childcare is more likely to decrease than to remain at no change among those furloughed. Additionally, when examining the effect of working from home in May 2020, we find that for men, when they are working from home, the gender gaps for meal and childcare are more likely to decrease than to remain at no change. For women, the gender gap for meal tends to increase than to remain at no change when their husbands are working from home. Regarding employment status, women in regular employment or nonregular/self-employment are less likely to witness an increase in gender gap in childcare than to remain at no change compared with those who are not employed.

To further examine relative resources, we focused on the effects of education and the wives' earnings ratio. Based on the responses of the men, we find that the gender gap for meal among couples in which only wives achieved college level education is more likely to decrease than to remain at no change compared with couples in which both spouses have the same level of education. Regarding the effect of the earnings ratio of the wives, when this ratio was greater than 20%, then the gender gaps for meal among female respondents and childcare among male respondents are more likely to decrease than to remain at no change.

In Table 3.3, we examine changes in gender gap at more than one year after the outbreak of the pandemic (from January 2020 to May 2021). We find that only a few

[4] Three properties, namely, consistency, normality, and efficiency of maximum likelihood estimation, which are used in multinominal logit models, have been proven to hold as the sample size approaches ∞ (Long, 1997). Although Long does not provide an absolute standard for sample size when applying the maximum likelihood estimation, he cites that estimation for data with less than 100 samples is risky and that estimation is adequate when the sample size is >500. In this sense, although the estimation of data with a relatively small sample size in this study is not necessarily inappropriate, one should note that the results of the analyses must be validated with other data in further studies.

Table 3.2 Results of multinominal logit models of changes in gender gap for housework and childcare during January and May 2020

	Meal		Meal		Childcare		Childcare	
	Women's response		Men's response		Women's response		Men's response	
Ref. no change	Increased	Decreased	Increased	Decreased	Increased	Decreased	Increased	Decreased
Respondents furloughed	1.147* (0.452)	−0.866 (0.704)	0.820 (0.854)	1.069 (0.671)	1.670* (0.790)	−0.083 (0.662)	0.224 (0.969)	2.027* (0.936)
Husbands working from home in May 2020	1.059** (0.399)	0.859† (0.511)	0.473 (0.683)	1.997** (0.662)	−1.489 (1.052)	0.755 (0.519)	-0.709 (0.979)	4.182** (1.254)
Wives' employment status (ref. not employed)								
Regular employment	0.070 (0.681)	−1.577 (0.958)			−2.436* (1.069)	−2.068† (1.108)		
Nonregular employment, or self-employed	−0.693 (0.482)	0.550 (0.629)			−2.497** (0.886)	−0.176 (0.577)		
Husbands' weekly work hour			−0.005 (0.029)	0.038 (0.024)			0.007 (0.023)	−0.029 (0.031)
Education (ref. both partners less than high school, or both partners college)								
Wife college, husband less than high school	0.748 (0.471)	−0.127 (0.707)	−0.613 (0.998)	1.573* (0.689)	1.429† (0.741)	−1.219 (1.087)	−0.080 (0.823)	−0.274 (1.247)
Wife less than high school, husband college	−0.775 (0.593)	−1.224 (0.823)	0.998 (0.739)	−0.146 (0.903)	0.018 (0.925)	−0.459 (0.639)	0.703 (0.941)	1.261 (1.058)

(continued)

Table 3.2 (continued)

	Meal		Meal		Childcare		Childcare	
	Women's response		Men's response		Women's response		Men's response	
Ref. no change	Increased	Decreased	Increased	Decreased	Increased	Decreased	Increased	Decreased
Ratio of wives' earnings (ref. less than 20%)								
20–50%	−0.247 (0.528)	1.256* (0.636)	0.241 (0.855)	0.810 (0.889)	0.378 (0.701)	0.331 (0.711)	0.692 (0.966)	3.762** (1.342)
More than 50%	−1.199† (0.682)	1.542* (0.769)	0.047 (0.890)	0.507 (0.730)	0.135 (0.956)	0.575 (0.990)	−0.175 (0.892)	2.598* (1.108)
N	252		159		185		115	
−2LL	331.88***		155.52***		206.28***		107.87***	
Pseudo R^2	0.141		0.236		0.268		0.350	

Notes † $p < 0.10$, * $p < 0.05$, ** $p < 0.01$. Standard errors are in parentheses. For "meal," models control for number of children, youngest child 6 years or younger, and respondent's and spouse's frequencies of "meal" in Jan. 2020. For "childcare," models control for number of children, and respondent's and spouse's frequencies of "childcare" in Jan. 2020

Table 3.3 Results of multinominal logit models of changes in gender gap for housework and childcare during January 2020 and May 2021

	Meal		Meal		Childcare		Childcare	
	Women's response		Men's response		Women's response		Men's response	
Ref. no change	Increased	Decreased	Increased	Decreased	Increased	Decreased	Increased	Decreased
Husbands working from home in May 2021	−1.709* (0.705)	−0.135 (0.445)	0.459 (0.741)	0.745 (0.657)	−0.279 (0.683)	−0.219 (0.617)	1.492† (0.883)	1.490 (0.917)
Wives' employment status (ref. not employed)								
Regular employment	0.488 (0.803)	0.621 (0.667)			−0.646 (0.915)	0.265 (0.855)		
Nonregular employment, or self-employed	0.579 (0.470)	0.398 (0.407)			−0.831 (0.608)	−0.940† (0.551)		
Husbands' weekly work hour			0.004 (0.019)	−0.007 (0.017)			0.013 (0.020)	−0.007 (0.021)
Education (ref. both partners less than high school, or both partners college)								
Wife college, husband less than high school	0.036 (0.543)	0.003 (0.476)	−0.832 (0.609)	−0.497 (0.523)	−0.049 (0.578)	−0.055 (0.560)	0.433 (0.754)	0.494 (0.769)
Wife less than high school, husband college	0.623 (0.527)	0.151 (0.452)	−0.089 (0.672)	0.248 (0.578)	0.902 (0.679)	0.870 (0.638)	0.185 (0.673)	−1.182 (0.829)

(continued)

Table 3.3 (continued)

	Meal		Meal		Childcare		Childcare	
	Women's response		Men's response		Women's response		Men's response	
Ref. no change	Increased	Decreased	Increased	Decreased	Increased	Decreased	Increased	Decreased
Ratio of wives' earnings (ref. less than 20%)								
20–50%	−0.463 (0.550)	0.140 (0.459)	0.861 (0.726)	1.406* (0.664)	0.674 (0.653)	−0.583 (0.686)	0.982 (0.755)	0.774 (0.798)
More than 50%	0.266 (0.767)	0.733 (0.650)	−0.623 (0.626)	0.162 (0.538)	−0.513 (0.783)	−1.176 (0.753)	−0.379 (0.631)	0.309 (0.664)
N	252		159		185		115	
−2LL	473.61***		297.34**		331.77***		201.40***	
Pseudo R^2	0.118		0.124		0.147		0.201	

Notes † $p < 0.10$, * $p < 0.05$, ** $p < 0.01$. Standard errors are in parentheses. For "meal," models control for number of children, youngest child 6 years or younger, and respondent's and spouse's frequencies of "meal" in Jan. 2020. For "childcare," models control for number of children, and respondent's and spouse's frequencies of "childcare" in Jan. 2020 factors related to the change. Husbands' working from home is less likely to increase than to remain at no change in relation to the gender gap for meal among women. When the earnings ratio of the wives is at 20%–50%, the gender gap for meal is more likely to decrease than to remain at no change for men. Apart from these factors, the study observed no significant associations with changes in the gender gap for meal and childcare for neither time availability nor relative resources. This suggests that the shift in gender gap for housework and childcare that occurred in approximately one year after the pandemic was not limited to a specific group. Instead, it occurred in a broad range of population.

3.7 Conclusion

Several issues related to the impact of the COVID-19 pandemic on the allocation of domestic labor need to be addressed. One of them is the question of whether or not the pandemic narrowed or widened the gender gap in domestic labor; if so, which factors are relevant? A few of the lifestyle changes due to the pandemic seemingly narrow down the gender gap in domestic labor (e.g., working from home for men), whereas others may have widened it (e.g., the detrimental effects on employment of women, which reduced their relative resources). This study described the changes in the frequencies of and spousal gender gap in housework and childcare for women and men since the outbreak of the pandemic. Furthermore, it explored the factors related to changes in the gender gap in domestic labor in terms of time availability and relative resources.

The second issue is whether or not the impact of the pandemic on the allocation of domestic labor changed over time. A few of the lifestyle changes triggered by the pandemic were contingent and temporary, whereas others remained altered and persistent. To clarify the trends over time, we examined the changes in spousal gender gap in domestic labor at three time points, namely, before the pandemic (January 2020), during the early stages of the pandemic (May 2020), and one year after the pandemic (May 2021), with partially relying on retrospective data. The following two points were identified based on the analyses of the two-wave social survey of married individuals aged 25–44 years with children.

First, the study observed no change in the gender gap in domestic labor for the majority of women and men in the early stages of the pandemic. Alternatively, the study noted a narrowing of the gender gap for 40–50% of the female and male respondents for housework and childcare one year after the outbreak of the pandemic. Evidently, even in May 2021, which is a little more than one year after the outbreak, a large gap remained in domestic labor between women and men, which hardly suggests that the gender gap in domestic labor for Japanese couples has been eliminated. However, the study infers that a sign of a decline in gender gap for domestic labor seemingly exists.

Second, time availability and relative resources were related to the changes in gender gap for domestic labor. The associations between these factors and changes in the gender gap, however, were more clearly observed in the early stages of the pandemic than one year after the outbreak. Specifically, during the early stages of the pandemic, men being furloughed reduced the gender gaps in housework and childcare, whereas women being furloughed increased these gender gaps.

The effect of husbands' working from home was seemingly ambivalent for gender gap during the early stage of the pandemic. Husbands' work from home reduced the gender gap in meals and childcare among male respondents, while it increased the gender gap in meals among female respondents. This suggests that there may be a discrepancy between wives' and husbands' perceptions of husbands' working from home. Even if husbands themselves felt that working from home allowed them to be more involved in housework and childcare, wives may have felt that their husbands being at home increased their domestic burden. Further studies are needed to examine the possibility that husbands' work from home has a different impact on wives and husbands, using matched data.

When women were employed, the gender gap in childcare was less likely to increase, and the economic resources of the women and being more educated than their husbands were associated with decreased gender gaps in housework and childcare.

Conversely, the study observed only a limited association between time availability, relative resources, and changes in the gender gap in domestic labor at approximately one year after the outbreak. In addition, we only partially observed that husbands' working from home was less likely to increase the gender gap in housework. Moreover, the modest economic power of the wives was more likely to reduce the gender gap in housework.

The result indicates the association between working from home for men and economic resources of women, although only partially, with changes in the gender gap at one year after the outbreak of the pandemic. These results suggest that continued working from home for men may facilitate their involvement in domestic labor, which may be due to the reduction of commute time and increased flexibility in time use, as well as due to their increased awareness of the need for domestic work by being at home. Notably, the economic resources of women can reduce the gender gap in domestic labor presumably by increasing their bargaining power. Meanwhile, the fact that the changes in the gender gap in domestic labor and its association with time availability and relative resources was relatively limited more than one year after the pandemic suggests that the shift toward the reduction of gender gap in domestic labor was not limited to certain groups of people. Instead, it occurred for a wider range of the population.

This study observed a narrowing of the gender gap in domestic labor one year after the outbreak of the pandemic. However, it is necessary to exercise caution and qualify such finding. One reason is that, as already noted, a significant difference is still evident between women and men in their frequencies of all the domestic tasks as of May 2021. Another reason is that the data used in this study relied on frequency to measure women's and men's domestic tasks. This may not adequately capture the increase in women's domestic labor during the pandemic. For example, this study fails to assess the extent to which the burden of childcare increased during the pandemic for women who were already taking care of their children "almost every day" before the pandemic. Therefore, changes in the gender gap in domestic labor during the pandemic need to be re-examined using different measures, such as time spent on housework and childcare.

This study also has several other limitations that should be noted. First, data were obtained from the same individuals at two time points after the outbreak of the pandemic; however, a part of the information was collected retrospectively. Thus, a possibility exists that the retrospective nature of the data may have led to measurement errors due to misremembering. Thus, the findings require revalidation with ongoing panel data since before the pandemic and based on the responses of the participants at the time of the survey. Second, the small sample size rendered the results less robust. Thus, the findings should be replicated using data from nationally representative and bigger sample sizes.

Despite these limitations, this study provides clues that the gender gap in domestic labor in the Japanese society may have shifted, albeit modestly, during the pandemic. Moreover, time availability for men and relative resources for women are relevant to this shift. This notion suggests a way forward for changes in gender inequality in the Japanese society. On the basis of these findings, research should be accumulated on whether or not and the manner in which the gender gap in domestic labor in the Japanese society may witness further changes.

Acknowledgements This work was supported by JSPS KAKENHI Grant Number JP18H00936.

References

Ando, J. (2012). Tomokasegi fuufu no kajiroudou koudou no henka (Changes in dual-earner couples' housework behavior: From the empirical analyses of cohort A in the JPSC. *Niigata Kokusai Jouhou Daigaku Jouhou Bunka Gakubu Kiyou (journal of Niigata University of International and Information Studies), 15*, 37–58.

Bae, J. (2009). Nihon to kankoku ni okeru dansei no ikuji sanka (Men's participation in child-rearing in Japan and Korea). *Keio Gijuku Daigaku Daigakuin Shakaigaku Kenkyuuka Kiyou* (*Studies in Sociology, Psychology and Education: Inquiries into Humans and Societies*), *68*, 59–73.

Brines, J. (1994). Economic dependency, gender, and the division of labor at home. *American Journal of Sociology, 100*(3), 652–688.

Carlson, D. L., Petts, R., & Pepin, J. R. (2021). Changes in US parents' domestic labor during the early days of the COVID-19 pandemic. *Sociological Inquiry, 92*(3), 1–28.

Chin, M., Sung, M., Son, S., Yoo, J., Lee, J., & Chang, Y. E. (2020). Changes in family life and relationships during the COVID-19 pandemic and their associations with perceived stress. *Family and Environment Research, 58*(3), 447–461.

Craig, L., & Churchill, B. (2021). Dual-earner parent couples' work and care during COVID-19. *Gender, Work, and Organization, 28*(S1), 66–79.

Del Boca, D., Oggero, N., Profeta, P., & Rossi, M. C. (2022). The impact of COVID-19 on the gender division of housework and childcare: Evidence from two waves of the pandemic in Italy. *IZA Journal of Labor Economics, 11*(1), 1–20.

Dunatchik, A., Gerson, K., Glass, J., Jacobs, J. A., & Stritzel, H. (2021). Gender, parenting, and the rise of remote work during the pandemic: Implications for domestic inequality in the United States. *Gender and Society, 35*(2), 194–205.

Hirai, M., & Watanabe, Y. (2021). Nyuyoji no chichioya ni okeru pandemic ni yoru hatarakikata no henka to kazoku to shigoto heno eikyo (The impact of COVID-19 on the family and working life of fathers with young children). *Shinrigaku Kenkyu (Japanese Journal of Psychology), 92*(5), 417–427.

Hupkau, C., & Petrongolo, B. (2020). Work, care and gender during the COVID-19 crisis. *Fiscal Studies, 41*(3), 623–651.

Ishibashi, S., Takeda, R., & Taniguchi, M. (2021). COVID-19 ga kosodate yushikisha no gender-gap ni oyoboshita eikyo: Kinkyujitai sengen mae/ chu/ go 3danmen deno kaji, ikuji jikan ni chakumoku site (Impact of Covid-19 on the gender gap among experts on child care: Focusing on housework and childcare time in three phases before, during, and after the declaration of a state of emergency). *Toshikeikaku Ronbun Shu (Journal of City Planning Institute of Japan), 56*(3), 641–648.

Ishii-Kuntz, M., & Coltrane, S. (1992). Predicting the sharing of household labor: Are parenting and housework distinct? *Sociological Perspectives, 35*(4), 629–647.

Kamo, Y. (1988). Determinants of household labor: Resources, power, and ideology. *Journal of Family Issues, 9*(2), 177–200.

Kamo, Y. (2000). "He Said, She Said": Assessing discrepancies in husbands' and wives' reports on the division of household labor. *Social Science Research, 29*(4), 459–476.

Kim, J., & Choi, Y. (2021). "코로나19 시기 가족관계 만족도 변화는 어떻게 설명할 수 있는가?: 남성 가사분담의 역할을 중심으로 (What enhances family relationship satisfaction during the COVID-19 pandemic?: The moderating influence of men's division of domestic labor). 비판사회정책 (*Journal of Critical Social Policy*), *70*, 101–132.

Kuroda, T. (2020). *Shingata korona no kagaku: Pandemikku, soshite kyousei no mirai he* (The science of the COVID-19: Pandemic and toward a future of co-existence). Chuokoron-Shinsya.

Long, J. S. (1997). *Regression models for categorical and limited dependent variables*. Sage Publications.

Lyttelton, T., Zang, E., & Musick, K. (2021). Telecommuting and gender inequalities in parents' paid and unpaid work before and during the COVID-19 pandemic. *Journal of Marriage and Family, 84*(1), 230–249.

Matsuda, S. (2000). Otto no kaji ikuji sanka no kitei youin (Husbands' participation in domestic work). *Nenpou Shakaigaku Ronshuu, 13*, 134–145.

Matsuda, S. (2006). Kinnen ni okeru chichioya no kaji ikuji sanka suijun to kitei youin no henka (The changes in fathers' participation in housework and childcare in recent years). *Kakei Keizai Kenkyuu (Japanese Journal of Research on Household Economics), 71*, 45–54.

Ministry of Internal Affairs and Communications, Japan. (2021). *Reiwa 3 nenban jouhou tsuushin hakusho* (White paper information and communications in Japan, 2021). Retrieved from https://www.soumu.go.jp/johotsusintokei/whitepaper/ja/r03/pdf/index.html. Accessed on 24 Nov 2022.

Ochiai, E., & Suzuki, N. (2020). COVID-19 kinkyuu jitai sengen ka ni okeru zaitakukinmu no jittai chousa: Kazoku oyobi gendaa he no kouka wo chuushin ni (Working from home during the COVID-19 pandemic: Results of a survey on the effects of staying at home on the family and gender relations in Japan). *Kyoto Syakaigaku Nenpou (Kyoto Journal of Sociology), 28*, 1–13.

Sasaki, S. (2018). Waaku raifu baransu jidai ni okeru dansei no kaji ikuji jikan no kitei youin tou ni kansuru jisshou bunseki (Determinant factors for time spent on housework by men). *Seikatsu Keizaigaku Kenkyuu (Journal of Household Economics), 47*, 47–66.

Sevilla, A., & Smith, S. (2020). Baby steps: The gender division of childcare during the COVID-19 pandemic. *Oxford Review of Economic Policy, 36*(Supplement_1), S169–S186.

Shafer, K., Scheibling, C., & Milkie, M. A. (2020). The division of domestic labor before and during the COVID-19 pandemic in Canada: Stagnation versus shifts in fathers' contributions. *Canadian Review of Sociology, 57*(4), 523–549.

Shelton, B. A., & John, D. (1996). The division of household labor. *Annual Review of Sociology, 22*, 299–322.

Statistics Bureau of Japan. (2022). *Reiwa 3 nen shakaiseikatu kihon chousa: Seikatsu jikan oyobi seikatsu koudou ni kansuru chousa, kekka no gaiyou* (Report of 2021 survey on time use and leisure activities). Retrieved from https://www.stat.go.jp/data/shakai/2021/pdf/gaiyoua.pdf. Accessed 10 Dec 2022.

Yokomaku, T. (2020). Kinkyuu jitai sengen ka ni okeru huuhu no kaji ikuji buntan (Sharing of housework and childcare for couples under a state of emergency). Mitsubishi UFJ Research & Consulting. Retrieved from https://www.murc.jp/wp-content/uploads/2020/05/survey_covid-19_200526.pdf. Accessed on 20 Jan 2021.

Zhou, Y. (2020). Shingata korona uirusu to koyou, kurashi ni kansuru NHK JILPT kyoudou chousa kekka gaiyou: josei no kibishii koyou joukyou ni chuumoku shite (Summary of the results from NHK/JILPT joint survey on COVID-19, employment, and living: Focusing on the severe employment situation of women). Retrieved from https://www.jil.go.jp/tokusyu/covid-19/collab/nhk-jilpt/docs/20201113-nhk-jilpt.pdf. Accessed on 20 Feb 2021.

Chapter 4
The Impact of the COVID-19 on Fertility in Eastern Asia: The Case of Japan

Nancy L. S. Leung, Takayuki Sasaki, and Shigeki Matsuda

Abstract This study aims to analyze the impact of the COVID-19 response policies on fertility in East Asia, particularly Japan, China, South Korea, Taiwan, and Hong Kong. In addition, this study takes Japan as a case study to examine the impact of the COVID-19 pandemic on pregnancy intention. The main results of the study are first, the COVID-19 response policies have suspended marriage events which proportionally affect fertility in most East Asian countries/region. In the case of South Korea and Hong Kong, decrease in international marriage due to border control push further decline in fertility. Second, although the COVID-19 response polices in Japan are self-sufficiency based, the self-guided policies imposed by different businesses have affected people's life in various ways, including childbearing-related facilities and services. Third, based on the data collected from the survey, pregnancy intention on second childbirth among married couples vary by respondents' age during the COVID-19 pandemic.

Keywords Eastern Asia · The COVID-19 response policies · Marriage and fertility · Pregnancy intention · Late childbearing

---

N. L. S. Leung (✉)
Nippon Sport Science University, Tokyo, Japan
e-mail: leung@nittai.ac.jp

T. Sasaki
Tsuda University, Tokyo, Japan

S. Matsuda
Chukyo University, Nagoya, Japan

S. Matsuda and H. Takenoshita (eds.), *Changes in Work and Family Life in Japan Under COVID-19*, Population Studies of Japan, https://doi.org/10.1007/978-981-99-5850-4_4

4.1 The COVID-19 in Eastern Asia

4.1.1 The Situation in 2020 and 2021

Taking a brief glance on the COVID-19 situation in Eastern Asia, a new contagious disease is found at Wuhan, the capital of Hubei Province in China in December 2019. In a short time, it spreads around China and near by countries. On 16 January 2020, Japan has announced the country's first infected case. 4 days later, on 20 January, Korea has announced the country's first infected case. Soon after that, Taiwan and Hong Kong have announced the first infected case on 21 January and 23 January respectively. All these infected cases are found from the person who has traveled to Wuhan. According to the World Health Organization (WHO), the number of newly infected cases in China has increased from 41 cases (12 January) to 147 cases (22 January), 3 times more in 10 days (World Health Organization, 2022). The Chinese government has imposed a lockdown policy at Wuhan on 23 January after the number of infected cases has increased sharply. However, the lockdown does not stop the spread of the disease, the number of infected cases in China further increases sharply to 2,590 cases 10 days after the lockdown (2 February). Based on the experiences with SARS and MERS, WHO takes a high concern on the disease and declares the disease is a "Public Health Emergency of International Concern" on 30 January. Later, WHO has named the disease as COVID-19 on 11 February and makes the assessment that COVID-19 can be characterized as a pandemic on 11 March (World Health Organization, 2020).

The situation of COVID-19 in Eastern Asia varies by country and region. Figures 4.1, 4.2, 4.3 and 4.4 show the daily newly confirmed COVID-19 cases in China, Japan, Korea, Taiwan, and Hong Kong between 3 January 2020 and 31 December 2021. Since the situation in 2022 is different to 2020 and 2021, the situation of 2022 will be discussed later. From Figs. 4.1, 4.2, 4.3 and 4.4, the waves of COVID-19 outbreak are different between countries and regions. Although the outbreak of COVID-19 in China is much earlier than other East Asian countries/regions, the number of confirmed cases remains less than 2000 after the peak in February 2020. This may be related to the China's COVID strategy, aiming to keep cases as close to zero as possible, namely "Zero-COVID Policy". Large-scale lockdowns, restrictions on internal and international traveling are imposed as soon as the outbreak of COVID-19 in Wuhan. Besides, China also imposes large-scale mass testing on COVID-19 and tracing infectors movement to track and stop the spread of the virus. Although the policy helps to keep the number of confirmed cases low, it has a huge impact on economy and people's daily life such as food shortage and global supply chain chaos.

Japan takes totally different stands in COVID-19 measures than other East Asian countries/regions. Although Japan has declared a "State of Emergency" on 7 April 2020 to stop the spread of COVID-19, the State of Emergency is not a restriction, rather it is just a "recommendation" and only applies in the prefectures with large number of COVID-19 infectors. The State of Emergency has once been expended as

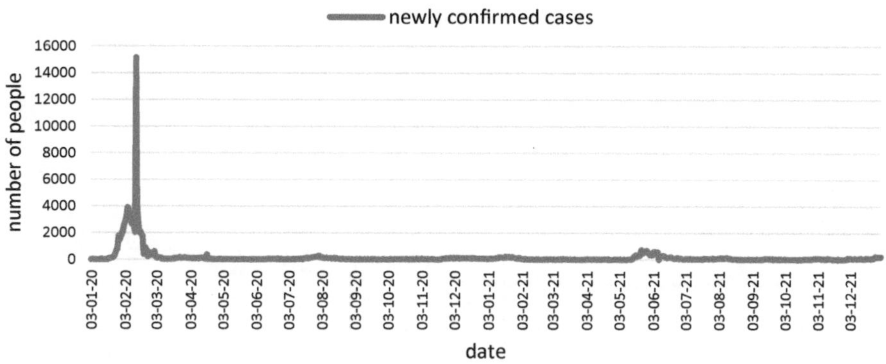

Fig. 4.1 Newly confirmed COVID-19 cases in China between 3 Jan 2020 and 31 Dec 2021. *Source* World Health Organization (2022)

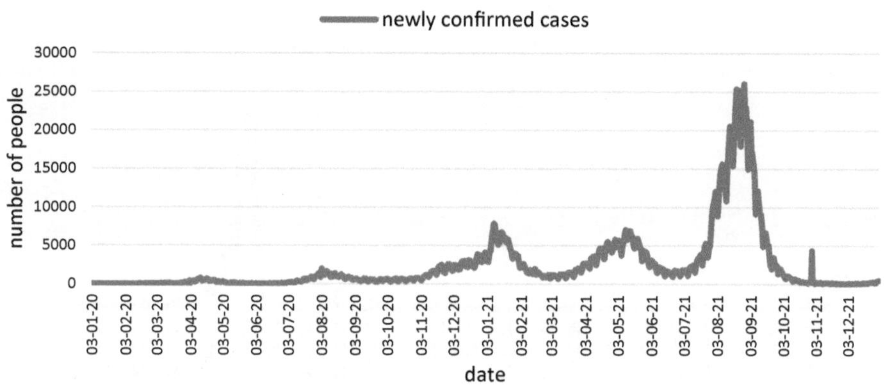

Fig. 4.2 Newly confirmed COVID-19 cases in Japan between 3 Jan 2020 and 31 Dec 2021. *Source* World Health Organization (2022)

a national wide COVID-19 measure in April 2020 and the only difference to other State of Emergency is just the request on school closures. Japan's COVID-19 measure mainly relies on citizens' self-decision, wearing mask, staying at home, beware of mass gathering, shorten business hours, etc., are all voluntary. The only restriction imposes to prevent the spread of COVID-19 is just international border controls for foreign travelers. The self-sufficiency-based "State of Emergency" gains success to prevent the spread of COVID-19, but the number of infectors increases sharply again when new variant appears in the society and resuming mass gathering events. This makes Japan faces several waves of COVID-19 infections between 2020 and 2021 (Fig. 4.2).

South Korea takes a more restricted stand on COVID-19 measures than Japan by imposing mass test, tracing and isolating COVID-19 infectors and restricting social distance. KI-Pass system is introduced to trace infectors who have visited public

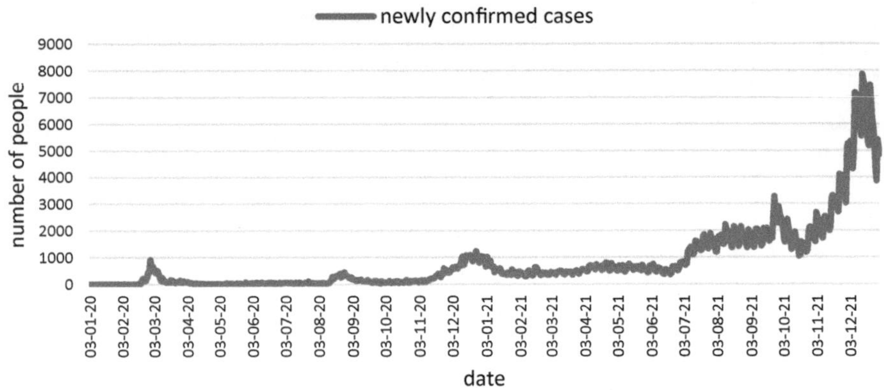

Fig. 4.3 Newly confirmed COVID-19 cases in South Korea between 3 Jan 2020 and 31 Dec 2021. *Source* World Health Organization (2022)

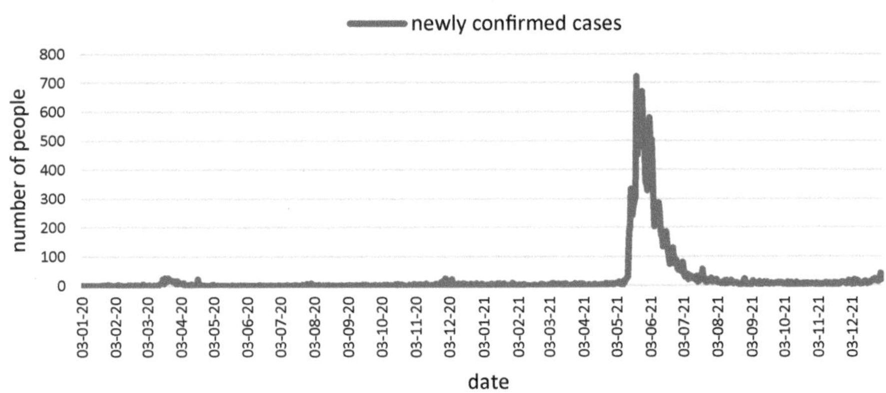

Fig. 4.4 Newly confirmed COVID-19 cases in Taiwan between 3 Jan 2020 and 31 Dec 2021. *Source* Taiwan National Infectious Disease Statistics System (2022)

facilities. Since the main source of spreading COVID-19 in South Korea is linked to religious group gathering, the levels of social distancing are prescribed in details (Ministry of Health & Welfare of Republic of Korea, 2020). However, at the end of 2021, there is an outbreak of COVID-19 cases in South Korea due to loosen restrictions, slow vaccination, and new variant appearance. Besides, South Korea also has imposed restrictions on international travels.

Taiwan takes a similar stand with South Korea on COVID-19 measures by leveling the status of COVID-19 spreading in society. Taiwan has imposed restrictions on wearing mask in public area, quarantine, cordon sanitaire, internal and international movement, mass testing and canceling or postponing large-scale events (Taiwan Centers for Disease Control, 2020). Taiwan has included lockdown policy in the COVID-19 measures when 100 new domestic COVID cases are found daily for 14 consecutive days, eventually it is not applied (Strong, 2021). The Taiwan COVID-19 measures gain a great success in controlling the spread of COVID-19 until May 2021, however after new COVID variant appears and low vaccination rate due to the shortage of vaccines, the number of infectors increase sharply. The reason for the shortage is not because Taiwan cannot pay for the vaccines; it is related to the relation between Taiwan and China. After Taiwan has rebuffed China's COVID vaccines offer, the Chinese company Fosun Pharma is claimed to have intervened the purchase deal between Taiwan and BioNTech (Taiwan News, 2021).

Hong Kong takes more intense COVID-19 measures than South Korea and Taiwan because of the SARS experiences in 2003. Since Hong Kong is an international transport hub, COVID-19 spreads quickly in Hong Kong by mainland visitors and hit the first wave in March 2020. Hong Kong immediately imposes restrictions on international travel and announces health quarantine arrangements on people arriving Hong Kong. Soon later, restrictions on physical gathering, dinning restrictions, closure of commercial facilities such as beauty parlors, public entertainment facilities, and school closures are also imposed. In November 2020, Hong Kong adopts the approach of achieving zero infection; a stricter guideline is further imposed. Like Taiwan, Hong Kong has imposed mass testing on infected districts or buildings; and like South Korea, Hong Kong has introduced "Health code scheme" to facilitate health declaration by QR code (The Government of the Hong Kong Special Administrative Region, 2020). Although Hong Kong has imposed intense COVID-19 measures, when the measures are being lifted or loosen, the number of infectors increases quickly due to low vaccination rate. In the case of Hong Kong, the low vaccination rate is not related to the supply of vaccines, rather it is related to the political events and distrust of the HKSAR government which goes along with the 2019–2020 Hong Kong protests (Fig. 4.5).

Table 4.1 has summarized the COVID-19 measures among the East Asian countries/regions during the most stringency period. Since Japan's COVID-19 measures are based on citizens' self-sufficiency, triangle is used rather than a tick. Figure 4.6

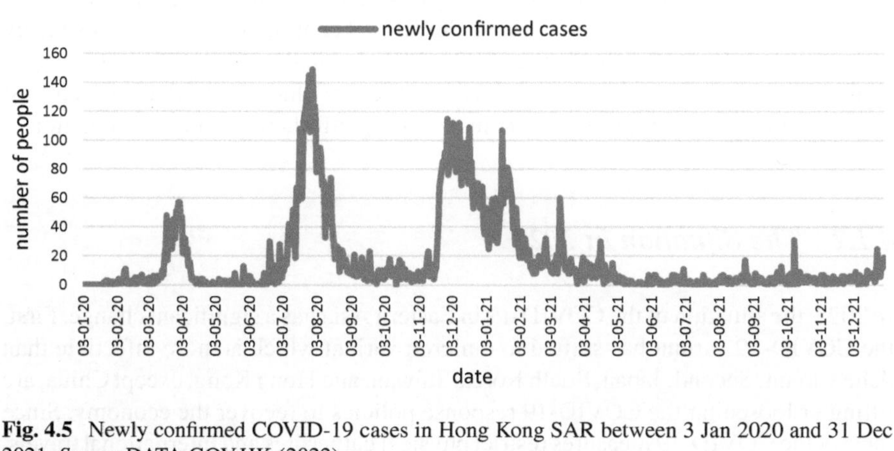

Fig. 4.5 Newly confirmed COVID-19 cases in Hong Kong SAR between 3 Jan 2020 and 31 Dec 2021. *Source* DATA.GOV.HK (2022)

Table 4.1 The policy responses to COVID-19 in East Asia

COVID-19 responses policies/countries	Japan	South Korea	China	Taiwan	Hong Kong
Lockdown (regional)			✓		
Lockdown (district)			✓		✓
School closures	✓	✓	✓	✓	✓
Public commercial facilities closures	△	✓	✓	✓	✓
Restrictions on mass gathering	△	✓	✓	✓	✓
Restrictions on concerts, sport games	△	✓	✓	✓	✓
Travel restrictions (international)	✓	✓	✓	✓	✓
Travel restrictions (domestic)	△		✓		
Mass testing		✓	✓	✓	✓
QR code tracking		✓	✓	✓	✓
Mandates to wear mask	△	✓	✓	✓	✓
Central quarantine		✓	✓	✓	✓
Home quarantine	△	✓	✓	✓	✓
Restrictions on visit hospital patient	△	✓	✓	✓	✓

Note ✓ measures implemented, △ measures loosely implemented
Source drawn by author based on the COVID-19 response policies of China, Japan, South Korea, Taiwan, and Hong Kong

shows the trend of OXFORD Government Response Stringency Index (OxCGRT) of the East Asian countries/regions between 2020 and 2021. From Table 4.1, the COVID-19 measures that are adopted by South Korea and Taiwan are almost the same but when comparing the stringency, South Korea has higher stringency than Taiwan (Fig. 4.6). Looking from the trend of the Index, it is clear that the East Asian countries/regions tighten or loosen the COVID-19 measures time by time. Between 2020 and 2021, China has the highest government response stringency on COVID-19 measures and Taiwan has the lowest. Among East Asian countries/regions, the level of government response stringency toward COVID-19 continues to increase as strategy of promoting COVID-19 vaccination is also included in the index. Since vaccination helps to reduce the risk of infection, death, and severe illness by COVID-19, all East Asian countries/regions governments make strong efforts to promote vaccination.

4.1.2 The Situation in 2022

In 2022, the situation of the COVID-19 in Eastern Asia has a significant change. First, the COVID-19 variant has shifted to omicron variant which is more infectible than delta variant. Second, Japan, South Korea, Taiwan, and Hong Kong, except China, are lifting or loosening the COVID-19 response policies to recover the economy. Since most of the COVID-19 measures restrict physical gatherings and international travels,

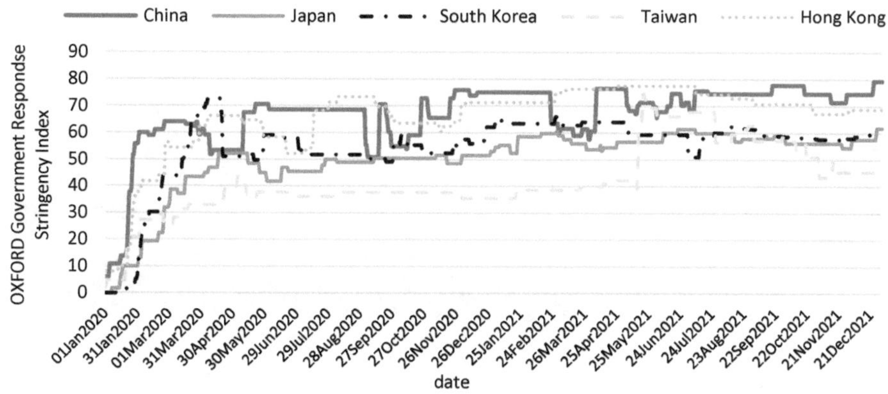

Fig. 4.6 The trend of OXFORD Government Response Stringency Index (2020–2021). *Source* HDX (2022)

it has great impact on hospitality industry. Hospitality industry is interconnected with multiple services, such as flights, food provider, and cleaning services. Figure 4.7 shows the changes of real GDP year on year by quarter. The growth of GDP during the COVID-19 pandemic period shrinks when the COVID-19 starts to spread in Eastern Asia. Except Taiwan, the changes of real GDP by quarter of China, Japan, South Korea, and Hong Kong have dropped below 0 in 2020. Although the level of shrink varies by country/region, it indicates that the COVID-19 pandemic has impact on the growth of GDP.

In 2022, for the sake of rebuilding the economy, Japan, South Korea, Taiwan, and Hong Kong are loosening or lifting the COVID-19 response policies even the number of infectors has increased sharply (Figs. 4.8, 4.9, 4.10, 4.11, and 4.12), which is 3–4 times more than 2020 and 2021. One of the reasons is the risk of severe illness and death of omicron variant is much lower than delta variant. Besides, COVID-19

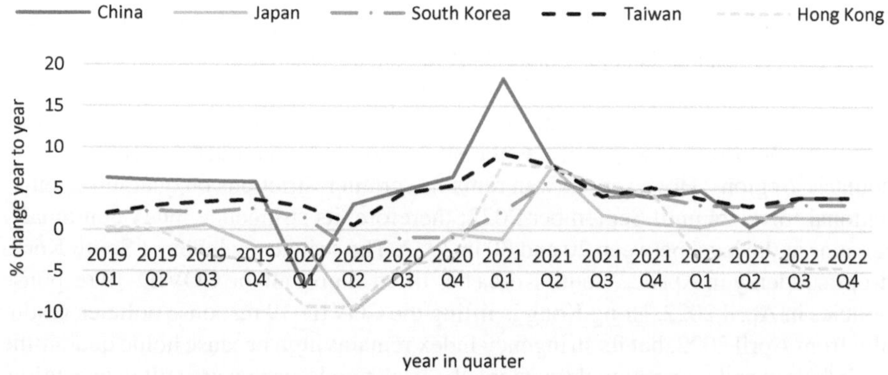

Fig. 4.7 Real GDP changes year on year by quarter (2019–2022). *Source* Bloomberg (2022)

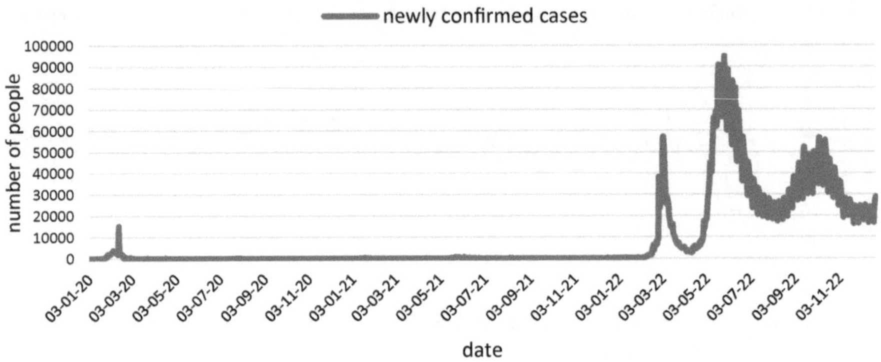

Fig. 4.8 Newly confirmed COVID-19 cases in China between 3 Jan 2020 and 23 Dec 2022. *Source* World Health Organization (2022)

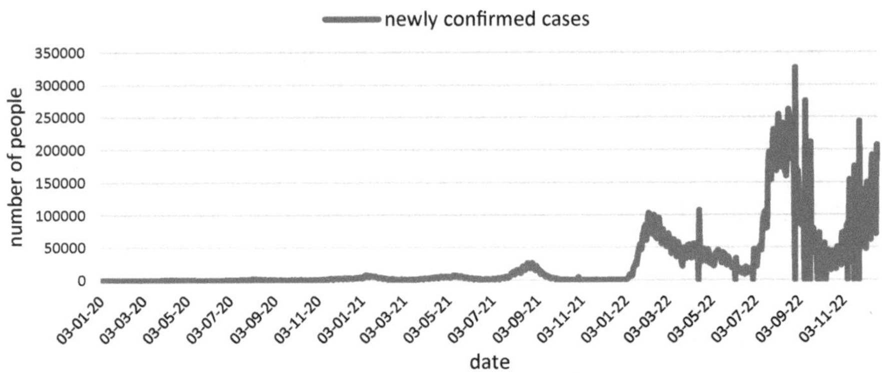

Fig. 4.9 Newly confirmed COVID-19 cases in Japan between 3 Jan 2020 and 22 Dec 2022. *Source* World Health Organization (2022)

antiviral oral drugs such as Paxlovid, Veklury, and Lagevrio are available in 2022 and it further helps to decrease the risk of death and severe illness.

Figure 4.13 shows the trend of the OxCGRT between 1 November 2021 and 6 November 2022. From Fig. 4.13, in Eastern Asia, Taiwan is the first one who lifts the COVID-19 response polices as the stringency index is much lower than other countries/regions. However, Taiwan remains certain restrictions on quarantine international travelers until September 2022; therefore, its stringency index continually remains at the level between 20 and 30 in 2022. The stringency index of South Korea drops suddenly in April as South Korea has lifted almost all the COVID-19 response policies in April 2022. Hong Kong is lifting the COVID-19 response policies gradually from April 2022, but its stringency index remains high because home quarantine for infectors and international travelers, the health code system are still in execution. Japan is lifting the COVID-19 response policies gradually, but the lifting is not as

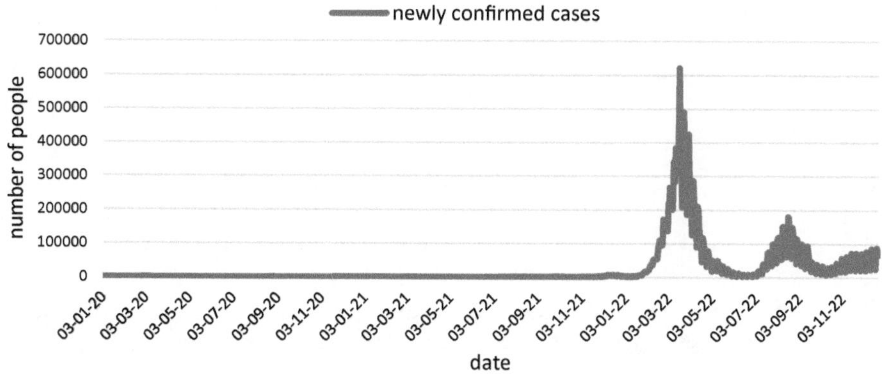

Fig. 4.10 Newly confirmed COVID-19 cases in South Korea between 3 Jan 2020 and 22 Dec 2022. *Source* World Health Organization (2022)

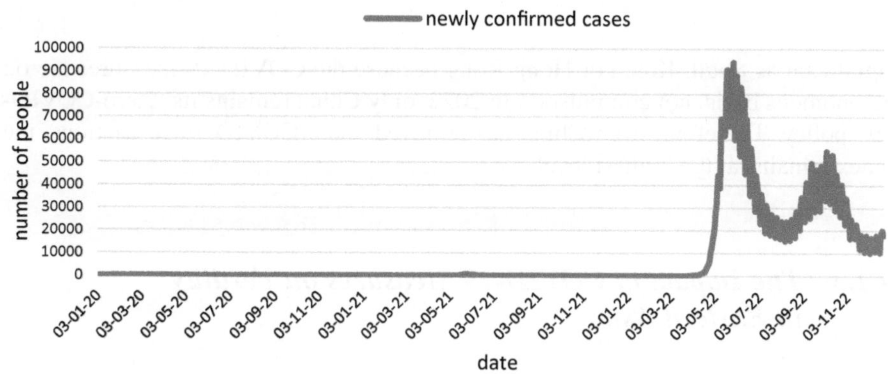

Fig. 4.11 Newly confirmed COVID-19 cases in Taiwan between 3 Jan 2020 and 23 Dec 2022. *Source* Taiwan National Infectious Disease Statistics System (2022)

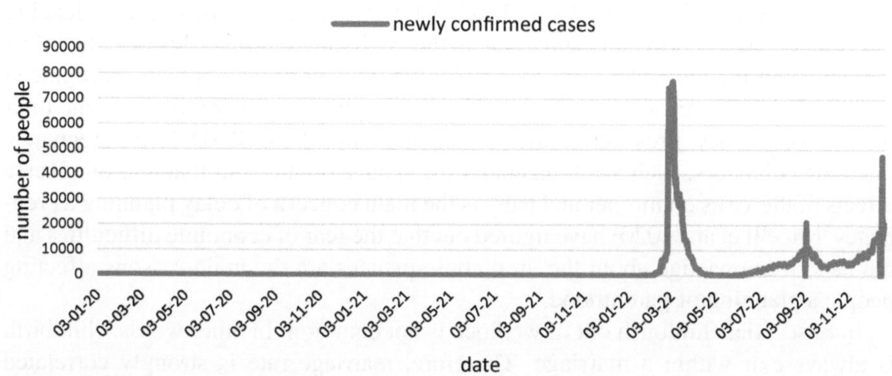

Fig. 4.12 Newly confirmed COVID-19 cases in Hong Kong between 3 Jan 2020 and 23 Dec 2022. *Source* DATA.GOV.HK (2022)

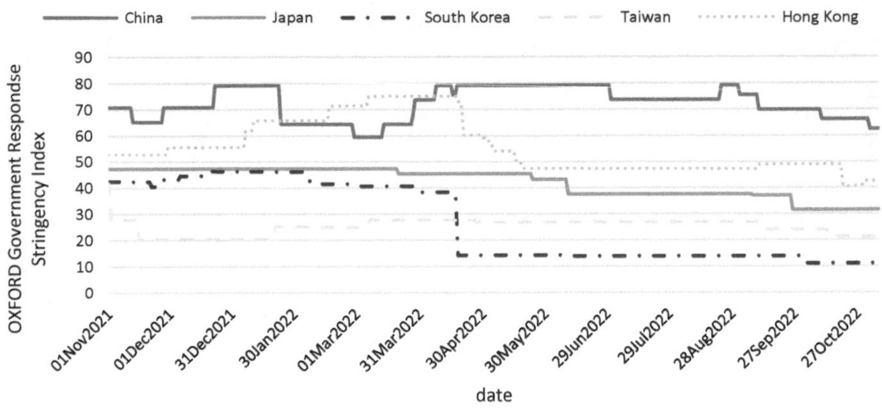

Fig. 4.13 The trend of OXFORD Government Response Stringency Index (1 Nov 2021–6 Nov 2022). *Source* HDX (2022)

significant as South Korea or Hong Kong because the COVID-19 measures are on autonomous basis, not compulsory. In 2022, only China remains its "Zero-COVID-19" policy. Therefore, even China has removed some COVID-19 restrictions, the index remains at the highest level.

4.1.3 The Impact of COVID-19 Measures on Fertility in Eastern Asia

Since the COVID-19 spreads around Eastern Asian, the total fertility rate (TFR) of these countries/regions shows a significant decrease, the most declining countries/regions during the COVID-19 pandemic is China, following by Hong Kong, and South Korea (Fig. 4.14). Since the COVID-19 is an unknown virus, misleading information are evolving and spreading at the beginning of 2020. Besides, the information about the unknown virus will affect the fetus or not is not being recognized in early 2020. Therefore, it is predictable that couples may delay or postpone their plan for pregnancy. Previous studies on the impact of the COVID-19 on pregnancy planning behaviors, such as Flynn et al. (2021) have pointed out that fear of adverse effects of the virus on mother and baby is the main concern of delay planning a pregnancy. Micelli et al. (2020) have figured out that the fear of economic difficulties and the lack of knowledge about the viral consequences are the main reasons affecting people's planning of parenthood.

In East Asia, childbirth out of wedlock is not common. In other words, childbirth is always exit within a marriage. Therefore, marriage rate is strongly correlated with fertility rate. Figure 4.15 shows the trend of crude marriage rate in East Asia between 2011 and 2021. During the COVID-19 pandemic, the marriage rate has significantly decreased, especially in 2020. The reasons for decreasing marriage rate

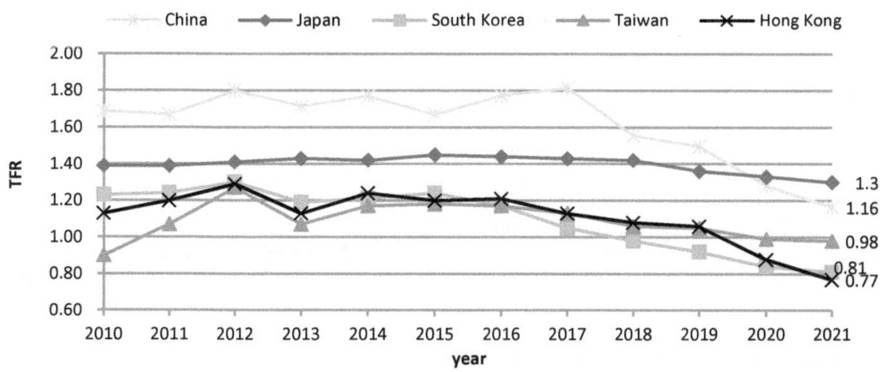

Fig. 4.14 The trend of total fertility rate of China, Japan, South Korea, Taiwan, and Hong Kong (2010–2021). *Source* China, United Nations (2022); Japan, Ministry of Health, Labour and Welfare of Japan (2022a; South Korea, Statistics Korea (2022); Taiwan, National Statistics Taiwan (2022); Hong Kong, Census and Statistics Department of the Hong Kong SAR (2022)

vary from country/region to country/region. For China, the restrictions on physical movement, especially lockdown, may lead to suspension of marriage registration. Besides, the lockdowns have led to shutdown of business operations and factories closure. This may affect certain people's income and lead to postpone marriage or childbearing. Furthermore, lockdown may suspend obstetrics and childbearing-related medical facilities. This may also affect couples' childbearing plan and leading to delay childbearing. In the study of Chen et al. (2022), women's intention of birth not only affected by the COVID-19, it is also affected by the economic uncertainity caused by the pandemic. Although China does not officially publish its TFR, the prospect from the "*World Population Prospects 2022*" published by UN Population Division may reflect the situation of China.

The case of Hong Kong is similar to China in certain ways. Although Hong Kong does not impose lockdown, restrictions on physical gathering have a strong impact on marriage event. The custom of marriage in Hong Kong usually consists of couples' parents and close relatives, such as grandparents, uncles, aunts, and their families. However, the physical gathering restrictions on marriage event sometimes limited to 20 people or sometimes even no food or drink should serve in the wedding ceremony or wedding banquet. Considering wedding banquet is a major event of the wedding, many couples delay their marriage because of the physical restriction which persuades a sharp decline in marriage rate during the COVID-19 pandemic. Furthermore, the cross-boundary marriage between Hong Kong resident and mainland Chinese resident is one of the major components of marriage in Hong Kong. Cross-boundary marriage must be registered either in Hong Kong or in mainland China in person. Border controls directly stop all the cross-boundary marriages as the couples cannot cross the border between Hong Kong and China. It seems that it is also a reason for the significant decline in marriage rate during the pandemic as births from cross-boundary marriage couples shares about 10% of the total births.

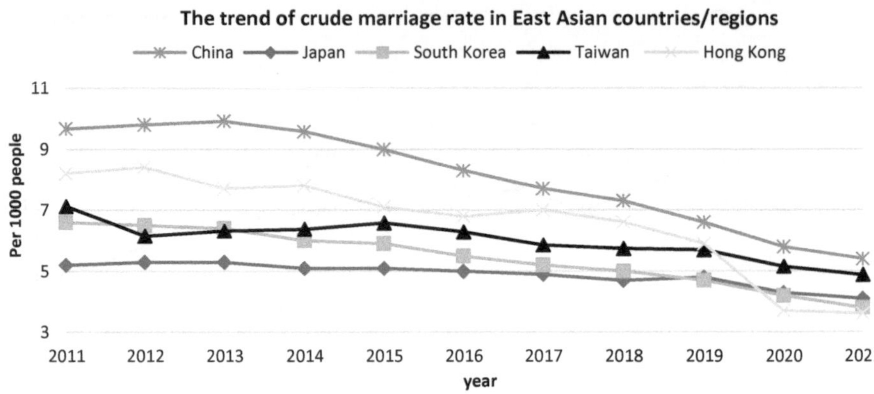

Fig. 4.15 The trend of crude marriage rate in East Asian countries/regions (2011–2021). *Source* China, Ministry of Civil Affairs of the People's Republic of China (2018, 2022); Japan, Ministry of Health, Labour and Welfare of Japan (2022a); South Korea, Statistic Korea (2022); Taiwan, National Statistics Taiwan (2022); Hong Kong, Census and Statistics Department of the Hong Kong SAR (2022)

The loss of the births from cross-boundary marriage is a main reason pushing Hong Kong's TFR further decline during the pandemic.

In the case of South Korea, the component of marriage is similar to Hong Kong because international marriage has a significant share. Since the number of international marriages of South Korea shares almost 10% (9.9% in 2019) of the total marriage (Statistic Korea, 2022a), the decrease in international marriage will directly affect the number of births from these couples. Besides, physical restrictions on gathering have influenced on traditional wedding events. Wedding is viewed as an important event between groom's and bride's extended family which is comparable to Hong Kong and China. Therefore, postponing wedding banquets is considered as one of the reasons leading to the decline in marriage rate and fertility rate (Kim & Kim, 2021).

In the case of Taiwan, international marriage shares about 10% (2019) of the total number of marriages and same as China, Hong Kong, and South Korea, border controls have decreased the number of international marriages during the COVID-19 pandemic. However, in general, the number of thc COVID-19 infectors and the impact of the COVID-19 on Taiwan's economy is much less than other East Asian countries/regions; therefore, the impact of the COVID-19 on fertility decline and decrease in marriage rate seems to be lower when comparing to other East Asian countries/regions.

In the case of Japan, although the COVID-19 pandemic has a great hit to Japanese economy, the decreasing trend of TFR and marriage rate during the COVID-19 pandemic is much gentle than other East Asian countries/regions. For the details, it will be discussed in the next section.

In sum, it can be said that the reasons of fertility decline during the COVID-19 pandemic in East Asia are first, the economic uncertainty causes by the COVID-19 responses policies such as lockdown, and business closure which directly stop or suspend people's daily economic activities. Second, border controls directly impede international marriages and leading countries/regions which have a high rate of international marriages to have further decrease in marriage rate and fertility rate, except Japan. Third, since most East Asian countries/regions view childbirth within wedlock is necessary and wedding event is an event that must associate with groom's and bride's extended families, physical restrictions on group gathering and business closures literally suspend marriages and leading to additional fertility decline.

4.2 COVID-19 and the Pregnancy Intension of Japan[1]

Japan has found the first COVID-19 infected cases on 16 January 2020 at Kanagawa prefecture, from a person who is back from Wuhan China. In 2020, Japan has faced 2 waves, one in April and one in July. Japan has declared the first "State of Emergency" on 7 April 2020. However, at the beginning this State of Emergency only applies on 7 prefectures and it becomes a national wide policy from 16 April. The State of Emergency includes some physical restrictions such as requesting people to stay at home, wearing mask, promoting teleworking, postponing not necessary traveling; some business closures, such as cinemas, libraries, department stores, schools, entertaining facilities which sells alcohol; and some recommendations on postponing large-scale events, such as concerts, sport games, conferences. Besides, the State of Emergency also requests restaurants and shops to shorten their business hours and not to provide alcohol in the evening. As mentioned in the previous section, the State of Emergency is voluntary or self-sufficiency based, not strongly restricted by laws, therefore, it all depends on the people. Between 2020 and 2021, Japan has declared 4 times State of Emergency, but only the first time is national wide, others are only in highly infected prefectures. And from the second "State of Emergency" (January–March 2021), the request on facilities closure is no longer exit, large-scale events, such as concerts, sport games, are allowed to conduct at half audience capacity. Although in the third State of Emergency, the request on large-scale events is tightened from half audience capacity to postpone or cancel, the main COVID-19 response policies remain on wearing mask, promoting teleworking, shortening public facilities' business hours and not to provide alcohol. And in the fourth State of Emergency, the request on large-scales events is backed to half capacity. In sum, the COVID-19 response policies that are adopted in Japan are not strongly restricting people's movement or gatherings; therefore, the impact on wedding events will be less when compare to China, South Korea, and Hong Kong. However, for the pregnancy intention, it is affected by many factors such as economic stability of the couple, income of the household, living environment, childbearing-related services, nursery services. Therefore, to measure the impact of the COVID-19 on pregnancy intention, it is necessary to examine what

[1] The content of this section is a reanalysis of the same data based on the analysis and results in the paper we published as Matsuda et al. (2022).

are the factors affecting couples' consciousness on childbearing. However, it is difficult to examine the impact of the COVID-19 pandemic on the first birth intention. It is because the consciousness on childbirth within wedlock is common in Japan and the first birth is always correlated to marriage. Since the marriage rate has significantly declined during the COVID-19 pandemic, it is believed that the intention of first birth will proportionally decrease. Table 4.2 shows the age of mother and the number of births by birth order between 2020 and 2021. It shows that during the COVID-19 pandemic, first birth has the largest decrease and followed by the second birth. However, the number of third birth or above does not have a decrease, rather it has increased. This implies that the COVID-19 pandemic does not have any influence on third birth pregnancy intention. Between 2020 and 2021, the number of first birth has reduced by 5.1%, and the number of second birth has reduced by 3.1%. Although the decrease in second birth is less than the first birth, the number of births has suggested that the COVID-19 pandemic does have some impact on second birth.

4.3 Data and Method

In November 2020, this research project has conducted a mail survey about work and life under the COVID-19 to examine the influence of the COVID-19 on family lives, specifically the life of family with one child and their further fertility intension. The survey is named "Survey on Work and Life under COVID-19," targeting married couples aged between 25 and 44 with at least one child. (For the details of the survey, please refer to Chap. 2).

In the survey, questions used to measure the pregnancy intention under the COVID-19 pandemic are (1) the desire number of children; (2) the actual number of children they have planned to have; and (3) any changes of their fertility plan under the COVID-19 pandemic. In the question asking about any changes of fertility plan, three possible answers are used to develop three groups of respondents: (1) "I want a further child and have rethink about the timing" ("postpone"); (2) "I want a further child and do not rethink about the timing" ("unaffected"); and (3) "I do not plan to have a further child" ("abandon").

For the sake of examining the impact of the COVID-19 pandemic on the pregnancy intention of family with children, a logistic regression analysis is used. Concerning that the pregnancy intention of those respondents who already have 2 or more children will be lower than those who only have one. The regression analysis only focuses on the respondents who only have one child. For the pregnancy intention, those who have "postpone" and "unaffected" their childbearing plan during the pandemic are counted as "intent to have further birth," those who have answered "abandon" are seen as "no intention to have further birth." In the logistic regression, respondent's age, working status, education level, and annual household income are the independent variables to examine the pregnancy intention under the COVID-19 pandemic. The age is continuous variable. Considering the possible economic effect of the COVID-19 pandemic, two dummy variables are used. They are the "double income (both

Table 4.2 The age of mother and the number of births by birth order (2020–2021)

Mother's age	2020				2021				Changes between 2020 and 2021			
	Total	1st birth	2nd birth	3rd birth or above	Total	1st birth	2nd birth	3rd birth or above	Total	1st birth	2nd birth	3rd birth or above
14 or below	37	36	1	–	32	32	–	–	△ 5	△ 4	△ 1	–
15–19	6,911	6,145	727	39	5,510	4,878	597	35	△ 1,401	△ 1,267	△ 130	△ 4
20–24	66,751	45,433	17,382	3,936	59,896	39,968	16,317	3,611	△ 6,855	△ 5,465	△ 1,065	△ 325
25–29	217,804	131,499	64,850	21,455	210,433	125,186	63,424	21,823	△ 7,371	△ 6,313	△ 1,426	368
30–34	303,436	127,490	121,936	54,010	292,439	122,733	117,022	52,684	△10,997	△ 4,757	△ 4,914	△1,326
35–39	196,321	64,437	79,939	51,945	193,177	62,506	77,678	52,993	△ 3,144	△ 1,931	△ 2,261	1,048
40–44	47,899	16,762	18,662	12,475	48,517	16,524	18,865	13,128	618	△ 238	203	653
45–49	1,624	697	523	404	1,597	595	535	467	△ 27	△102	12	63
50 or above	52	39	8	5	20	11	6	3	△ 32	△ 28	△ 2	△ 2
Total number	840,835	392,538	304,028	144,269	811,622	372,434	294,444	144,744	△ 29,213	△ 20,104	△ 9,584	475

Source Portal Site of Official Statistics of Japan (2022)

husband and wife have work and income)" and "household income." In terms of household income, according to the latest "Comprehensive Survey of living Conditions 2019," the average household income for household with children is about 75 million yen in 2018 (Ministry of Health, Labour & Welfare of Japan, 2020), therefore, the household income variable is set at reaching 75 million yen or not. There are two more dummy independent variables which is usually used in examining pregnancy intention, they are the working status ("full-time worker") and education background ("graduate or above"). It is because full-time working in Japan implies a stable income and less affected by layoffs during financial distress. And for the education background, since higher educated people seem to delay fertility due to their career path or concern more on the quality and quantity of their children, they may be affected by the COVID-19 pandemic by time factor rather than economic factor.

4.4 Result

Table 4.3 shows the distribution of respondents by the number of children in the family. Most of the respondents already have two children (57.0%) or three children (21.9%). Family with one child only share 16.1%.

From the result of the questions about ideal number of children and actual number of children, there is a trend that respondents plan to have less children than their ideal number (Table 4.4). And having two children seems to be the most ideal.

Since having two children is the most ideal, respondents who have only one child may have a higher intention in having a further child than those who have two or three children. Thus, the following analysis on pregnancy intention will mainly focus on the respondents who only have one child. The number of respondents who only have one child is 101. Looking at their age-range, most of them are in their late 30s and early 40s (Table 4.5). The distribution of respondents' education background is mainly on university graduate (27.7%), followed by high school (22.8%) and vocational college (21.8%) (Table 4.6). For the employment situation under the COVID-19 pandemic, although the percentage of full-time working has decreased, over half of the respondents work full-time before or during the COVID-19 pandemic (Table 4.7).

Table 4.3 The number and share of respondents by the number of children

Number of children	Number of respondents	% in total
1	101	16.1
2	357	57.0
3	137	21.9
4	23	3.7
5 or above	8	1.3
Total	626	100

Table 4.4 The number and percentage of respondents by the ideal and actual number of children

Number of child/children	Ideal number of children		Actual number of children	
	Number of respondents	%	Number of respondents	%
0	2	0.3	0	–
1	29	4.6	66	10.5
2	333	53.2	352	56.2
3	222	35.5	166	26.5
4	24	3.8	27	4.3
5 or above	9	1.4	7	1.1
No answer	7	1.1	8	1.3
Total	626	100.0	626	100.0

Table 4.5 The number and percentage of respondents by age ranges

Age-range	Number of respondents	% in total
25–29	7	6.9
30–34	27	26.7
35–39	32	31.7
40–44	35	34.7
Total	101	100

Table 4.6 The number and percentage of respondents by education background

Education background	Number of respondents	% in total
High school	23	22.8
Vocational college	22	21.8
Junior college	18	17.8
University	28	27.7
Graduated school	5	5.0
No answer	5	5.0
Total	101	100

In order to reveal the pregnancy intention under the COVID-19 pandemic, logistic regression is done with independent variables age, double income family or not, working situation, education background, and household income. The result is shown in Table 4.8. Age and education background have impact on respondents' pregnancy intention during the COVID-19 pandemic. And age is the main factor affecting people's pregnancy intention. The reason of age may relate to the childbearing age. According to the American Centers for Disease Control and Prevention (CDC), the standard age range for childbearing or childbearing potential is often ages 16–49 (Centers for Disease Control and Prevention, 2013). And it is a common knowledge also in Japan that the risk of having gestational hypertensive disease, gestational

Table 4.7 The number and percentage of respondents by working situations

Timing	(January 2020)		(May 2020) (First "State of Emergency")	
Employment situation	Number of respondents	% in total	Number of respondents	% in total
Full-time employment	61	60.40	57	56.44
Part-time employment	19	18.81	20	19.80
No job	21	20.79	20	19.80
Job hunting	–	–	1	0.99
No answer	–	–	3	2.97
Total	101	100.00	101	100.00

Table 4.8 The result of the logistic regression on pregnancy intention

Independent variables	β	SE	Wald	Df	*p*-value	Exp(B)
Age	−0.273	0.062	19.302	1	0.000***	0.761
Double income (dummy)	−0.082	0.579	0.020	1	0.887	0.921
Full-time worker (dummy)	0.079	0.529	0.022	1	0.882	1.082
Graduate or above (dummy)	1.209	0.528	5.237	1	0.022*	3.351
Annual income less than 75 million yen (dummy)	−0.921	0.566	2.649	1	0.104	0.398
Constant	10.067	2.526	15.882	1	0.000	23,559.615

Note *** $p < 0.01$, * $p < 0.05$

diabetes, placental abruption, placenta praevia, perinatal death, preterm labor, fetal macrosomia, and fetal growth restriction increases when childbearing age goes over 35 years. Besides, the risk for the baby to have Down syndrome increases 10% when childbearing age goes over 40. Therefore, the age of mother is very important not only to her own health, but also to her baby (Walker & Thornton, 2016). Therefore, to avoid the risk of childbearing at above 35 years, most couples try to have their second child before mother turns 35. In the survey, the age of respondents who have one child mostly at their late 30s or early 40s and over half of the respondents are female.[2] This implies that most of them are in the late childbearing age and time factor is the concern for future childbearing.

Another factor affecting respondents' pregnancy intention is educational background, especially university graduate. This may also relate to present situation in Pacific Asia which higher educated people, especially women tend to get married later and relatively delay childbearing (Jones, 2007). Therefore, couples' education background as a factor affecting pregnancy intention also relates to the age factor.

[2] Within 101 respondents who have one child, 45.5% are male and 54.5% are female.

On the contrary, from the regression result, double income, household income, working situation, in other words, economic factors do not show any significant relation to pregnancy intention. This may be because Japanese government has provided certain types of subsidies to maintain the living of low-income households, businesses, or industries which are affected by the COVID-19 pandemic. For example, "Temporary Loan Emergency Funds" for the households who face economic problem due to temporary unemployment or unpaid pandemic leave (Ministory of Health, Labour and Welfare of Japan, 2021); and "Kyugyou shien kin" (Fund for business closure) which provide financial support for the businesses which have cooperated with the government to temporary close their business (Ministry of Health, Labour and Welfare of Japan, 2022b). Furthermore, looking from the unemployment rate, although the rate during the COVID-19 pandemic has increased from 2.4% (2019) to 2.8% (2020), it is lower than 2016 (3.1%) or before (Portal Site of Official Statistics of Japan, 2022). In other words, the COVID-19 pandemic does not have much influence on employment. However, the unemployment rate does not include those who are required to have unpaid pandemic leave. It is believed that the economic impact on nonregular workers is much more than regular workers.

4.4.1 Reviewing Japan's Low Fertility from the COVID-19 Pandemic

During the COVID-19 pandemic, the TFR of Japan shows a declining trend, however, the decline is slightly. This may relate to the self-sufficiency based COVID-19 response polices that allow most of the business operations and people's daily life can maintain at a certain level during the pandemic. Since Japan did not impose lockdown policy or strongly restrict physical movement, there should be no difficulty to access pregnancy check-up or obstetrics.

However, from the survey, 13 respondents (family with one child) have provided reasons of postponing childbearing. One of the reasons is, finding difficulties to access pregnancy check-up. A similar reason of postponing childbearing which is related to medical facilities is husband is not allowed to stay at the delivery room during childbirth. In April 2020, the Japan Association of Obstetricians and Gynecologists has issued a notice to pregnant women, which aims to provide medical information for pregnant women during the COVID-19 pandemic. In this notice, it has mentioned that the frequency of pregnancy check-up may decrease due to the situation of COVID-19 and the delivery method is aggressively shifting to cesarean section, C-section (Japan Association of Obstetricians & Gynecologists, 2020). This explains why the difficulty of pregnancy check-up is one of the reasons postponing childbearing. Although the Japanese government did not impost any restrictions on accessing hospitals or obstetrics, hospitals and obstetrics voluntarily impose restrictions on access. Besides, basically in Japan, pregnant women are not allowed to choose birth delivery method. The most common method is vaginal delivery and C-section only applies to those who are not suitable for vaginal delivery such as abnormal presentation, placenta problems, large baby weighing. Vaginal delivery is not covered by medical insurance, but C-section is covered. Even though medical insurance is applicable, the cost of C-section is still much higher than vaginal delivery. Furthermore, in many countries, such as America, spouse or partner is allowed to enter the delivery room with pregnant mother even during C-section. In Japan, spouse is only allowed to enter delivery room during vaginal delivery. Yet, during the COVID-19 pandemic, most of the countries have restricted spouse entering delivery room due to restricted infectivity. Therefore, even Japan does not have strong restrictions on physical movement or business operation, the self-directed responses on preventing the spread of the COVID-19 by medical facilities have generated uncertainty on the frequency pregnancy check-up and higher cost of delivery method which affect couples' pregnancy intention.

In addition, respondents have mentioned some economic factors affecting their pregnancy intention. The economic factors which have mentioned are changes in usual daily practice, insecure income, and risk of layoff. Although in the result of logistic regression, economic factors do not show any significant relation to pregnancy intention, the COVID-19 pandemic does affect people's daily life in certain ways, especially in 2020. At the beginning of the COVID-19 outbreak, information about the new disease was unaccounted which leading lots of rumors circulating in social media. Soon, following the international border control, international logistics, supply chains are all affected and standstill. This leads to rising prices in imported goods, and further leading to increasing prices in foods, living wares, energy related utilities costs. These changes directly affect people's daily life and household expenditure plan. Furthermore, international border control directly hit the hospitality industry such as tourist sites, restaurants, hotels. People who are working at hospitality industry may face unpaid pandemic leaves, temporary unemployment or even layoff which lead to concerns of insecure income and risk of layoff. However, as mentioned above, the unemployment rate in Japan has remained low even during the COVID-19 pandemic and various financial supports are provided by the Japanese government which helps Japanese to maintain their living and business. Thus, it is not surprised to find the regression result shows no relation between economic factor and pregnancy intention.

In fact, most of the respondents have pointed out that the main reason to postpone childbearing is the concern of infection. Since the survey was done in November 2020 and the COVID-19 vaccine was not yet produced, it is believed that infection was the main reason of postponing childbearing in 2020. However, from the result of this research, those who are in their late 30s or early 40s and willing to have further births and may keep their childbearing plan as the concern on childbearing time limitation is bigger than the risk of infection. Nonetheless, the concern on infection is being reduced when the COVID-19 vaccine is administered worldwide, and the risk of death and severe illness are much lower after omicron variant has replaced delta variant as the mainstream in 2021.

All in all, the case of fertility decline under the COVID-19 pandemic has indicated that childbearing age is the main factor affecting couples' pregnancy intention.

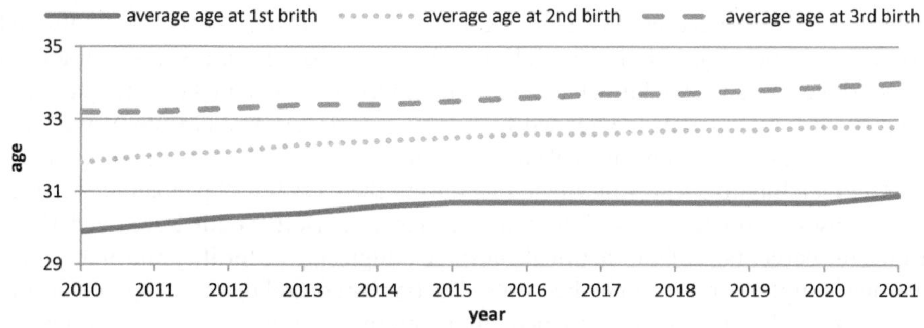

Fig. 4.16 The trends of mother's average age at birth by birth orders (2010–2020). *Source* Ministry of Health, Labour and Welfare (2022a)

Women in their late 30s and early 40s are still willing to have further births even under the pandemic. In other words, there is a demand of childbearing for women who are in their late 30s and early 40s. Late childbearing is a global trend as women tend to have more education and work experience before childbearing. Japan also has the same situation as the average age of mother at different birth orders has increased. For the first birth, it has reached 30.9 and the second birth has reached 32.8 (Fig. 4.16). This implies that most women in Japan start their childbearing after aged 30. Since late childbearing is riskier than childbearing in 20s, providing extra supports for late childbearing women such as "cryopreservation," "pre-pregnancy check-up," "assisted reproductive technique" may help to recover Japan's fertility.

4.5 Conclusion

This chapter has analyzed the COVID-19 response policies in Eastern Asia and examined its impact on fertility decline. Furthermore, this study has picked up Japan as a case to study the impact of the COVID-19 on pregnancy intention and reviews Japan's the fertility decline. In the part of analyzing the COVID-19 response policies in Eastern Asia, the study has figured out that China has the most restricted polices, and Japan has the loosest policies. And the stringency of the COVID-19 response policies has a parallel relationship with the rate of fertility decline. Since birth withing wedlock is the common sense in Eastern Asia, the impact of the COVID-19 response policies on marriage also influence fertility. In other words, marriage rate and fertility rate are corelated in Eastern Asia. This study has pointed out that the long-term lockdown in China not only has disputed the legal procedure of marriage, obstetrics and childbearing related medical facilities are all affected. The lockdown also suspends most of the business operations and manufacture which affect most people's income and further leading to delay of marriage and childbearing.

Other than China, the other East Asian countries/regions does not impose lockdown policies. However, a significant decline in marriage rate and fertility rate has appeared in South Korea and Hong Kong. One of the reasons is the traditional approach on marriage. China, South Korea, and Hong Kong share a similar tradition in marriage, which is wedding banquet is an important event and the participation of both groom's and bridge's extended families is necessary. The closure of wedding venues and restrictions on physical gatherings have suspended marriage related activities and leading to a lower marriage rate during the COVID-19 pandemic. Another main reason is related to the international marriage. Both South Korea and Hong Kong, the percentage of international marriage is high and the fertility rate of the international couples is higher than the locals. The border control that has imposed during the COVID-19 pandemic has stopped all the international marriage and leading to a further decrease in marriage and fertility and pushing the fertility rate to historical low in both South Korea and Hong Kong.

On the contrary, Japan has the loosest policies toward the COVID-19 and the decline rate in marriage and fertility are the least among the East Asian countries/regions. The reason why Japan has the loosest measures is the policies are self-sufficiency based. Although the COVID-19 response policies are not strongly restricted, most of the commercial facilities follow the recommendations and shorten the business hours, limit the audience capacity, or postpone events. Therefore, it can be said that the decrease in marriage rate and fertility is not directly affected by the official COVID-19 response policies, rather they are affected by the self-directed policies imposed by the society.

In terms of the loss of economy, all countries face a serious loss during the first-time outbreak of the COVID-19. Although the impact of the COVID-19 pandemic on economy varies from country/region to country/region, when more detailed information about the COVID-19 and vaccines are available in 2021, the damage on economy is relieved. At the same time, the restrictions on physical gathering have gradually loosed or lift.

In the second part of this study, the focus is on Japan and the impact of the COVID-19 pandemic on pregnancy intention. Although Japan has imposed a "State of Emergency," all the policies are recommendations rather than restrictions. Yet, most of the commercial facilities, businesses have imposed a self-guided policies to prevent the spread of the virus. Therefore, the State of Emergency does not have much influence on people's living, but the self-based policies have more impact on people's life. The result from the data analysis has pointed out that "age" is the main factor affecting people's second child pregnancy intention during the COVID-19 pandemic. It is because there is an age limitation in childbearing. Standard childbearing age range is between 15 and 49, after 35, the risk of having gestational hypertensive disease, gestational diabetes, placental abruption, placenta praevia, perinatal death, preterm labor, fetal macrosomia, and fetal growth restriction will increase, and after 40, the risk for the baby to have Down syndrome will increase 10% comparing to mothers in 20s or 30s. Therefore, age of the mother is an important factor toward childbearing. Besides, education background, especially university graduate has impact on pregnancy intention during the COVID-19 pandemic. It may because higher educated women tend to delay marriage and childbearing. Therefore, concerning the risks of late childbearing, those higher educated women who have reached certain age choose not to postpone their childbearing plan even under the COVID-19 pandemic.

In addition, the result of the survey has pointed out 2 main reasons postponing couples' second childbearing plan during the COVID-19 pandemic. First, concerns on accessing obstetrics and related medical facilities. As mentioned above, Japanese government does not impost any restrictions on physical movement, hospitals or obstetrics clinics have imposed their own policies on preventing the COVID-19 and these policies include reducing the frequency of pregnancy check-up and delivery method is being limited to C-section. Second, economic uncertainty. Although the unemployment rate in Japan during the COVID-19 pandemic remains low, self-directed business closure forcing employee to have unpaid pandemic leaves or even temporary unemployment. Especially during the COVID-19 pandemic, almost all countries have imposed border control and do not allow international travel, this policy hit heavily on hospitality industry. Therefore, even the Japanese unemployment rate is low, it is believed that most of the employees who belong to hospitality industry have to take unpaid pandemic leave or facing temporary unemployment and affecting their income. Though, the regression result shows economic factor does not affect couples' pregnancy intention during the COVID-19 pandemic.

The results also suggest that there is a demand of childbearing among late 30s and early 40s women. These age range is seen as late childbearing and usually have higher risk during their pregnancy. However, if the women from late 30s or early 40s are willing to give birth, it will help fertility to recover. In other words, introduce supporting late childbearing services may help to recover Japan's fertility.

To conclude, the impact of COVID-19 on fertility decline in Eastern Asia varies countries/region to countries/region, but the correlation between marriage and fertility is reconfirmed. In the case of Japan, under the COVID-19 pandemic, "age" of the women is the main factor affecting couples' second child pregnancy intention. Although the data used in this study is limited to married couples with at least one child, it indicates that certain couples are willing to have their second child even mother is in late childbearing age. Thus, introduce supportive services for late childbearing may help to recover Japan's fertility.

References

Bloomberg, L. P. (2022). *China, Japan, South Korea, Taiwan, Hong Kong real quarterly GDP.* Retrieved Decemeber 30, 2022, from Bloomberg terminal.

Centers for Disease Control and Prevention. (2013). *Adjusting national health and nutrition examination survey sample weights for women of childbearing age.* Retrieved December 26, 2022, from National Center for Health Statistics https://www.cdc.gov/nchs/data/series/sr_02/sr02_157.pdf

Chen, T., Hou, P., Wu, T., & Yang, J. (2022). The impacts of the COVID-19 pandemic on fertility intenstion of women with childbearing age in China. *Behaviorla Sciences, 12*(9). https://doi.org/10.3390/bs12090335

DATA.GOV.HK. (2022). *Data in Coronavirus disease (COVID-19).* Retrieved December 26, 2022, from DATA.GOV.HK https://data.gov.hk/en-data/dataset/hk-dh-chpsebcddr-novel-infectious-agent

Flynn, A., Kavanagh, K., Smith, A., Poston, L., & White, S. (2021). The impact of the COVID-19 Pandemic on Pregnancy Planning Behaviors. *Women's Health Reports, 2*(1), 71–77. Retrieved 12 29, 2022, from https://doi.org/10.1089/whr.2021.0005

HDX. (2022). *OXFORD COVID-19 government response stringency index.* Retrieved 12 29, 2022, from The Humanitarian Data Exchange https://view.officeapps.live.com/op/view.aspx?src=https%3A%2F%2Fraw.githubusercontent.com%2FOxCGRT%2Fcovid-policy-tracker%2Fmaster%2Fdata%2Ftimeseries%2FOxCGRT_timeseries_all.xlsx&wdOrigin=BROWSELINK

Japan Association of Obstetricians and Gynecologists. (2020). *COVID-19 related information.* Retrieved January 3, 2023, from To pregnancy women https://www.jaog.or.jp/wp/wp-content/uploads/2020/04/200407.pdf

Jones, G. (2007). Delayed marriage and very low fertility in Pacific Asia. *Population and Development Review, 33*(3), 453–478. Retrieved December 28, 2022, from https://onlinelibrary.wiley.com/doi/epdf/10.1111/j.1728-4457.2007.00180.x

Kim, J., & Kim, T. (2021). Family formation and dissolution during the COVID-19 pandemic: Evidence from South Korea. *Global Economic Review, 50*(1), 1–19. Retrieved December 26, 2022, from https://doi.org/10.1080/1226508X.2021.1874466

Matsuda, S., Sasaki, T., & Leung, L. S. N. (2022). Impact of the COVID-19 pandemic on birth planning in Japan. *Sociological Theory and Methods, 37*(1), 106–123. https://doi.org/10.11218/ojjams.37.106

Micelli, E., Cito, G., Cocci, A., Polloni, G., Russo, G. I., Minervini, A., Carini, M., Natali, A., & Coccia, M. E. (2020). Desire for parenthood at the time of COVID-19 pandemic: An insight into the Italian situation. *Journal of Psychosomatic Obestetrics & Gynecology, 41*(3), 183–190. Retrieved December 19, 2022, from https://doi.org/10.1080/0167482X.2020.1759545

Ministory of Health, Labour and Welfare of Japan. (2021). *Guidance on temporary loan emergency funds.* Retrieved December 28, 2023, from https://corona-support.mhlw.go.jp/seikatsufukushi/en/index.html

Ministry of Civil Affair of the People's Republic of China. (2018). *Civil affair statistics 2017.* Retrieved December 26, 2022, from https://www.mca.gov.cn/article/sj/tjgb/201808/20180800010446.shtml

Ministry of Civil Affaris of the People's Republic of China. (2022). *Civil affaris statistics 2021.* Retrieved December 26, 2022, from https://www.mca.gov.cn/article/sj/tjgb/202208/20220800043589.shtml

Ministry of Health and Welfare of Republic of Korea. (2020). *All about Korea's response to COVID-19.* Retrieved December 29, 2022, from Coronavirus (COVID-19), Republic of Korea https://is.kdca.go.kr/covid19_is/nCnvAdmin/modules/download.jsp?BOARD_ID=14&CONT_SEQ=3855&FILE_SEQ=5298

Ministry of Health, Labour and Welfare of Japan. (2020). *Income etc. of various types of households.* Retrieved December 26, 2022, from Summary Report 2019 https://www.mhlw.go.jp/english/database/db-hss/xls/2019-02Income-TablesFigures.xlsx

Ministry of Health, Labour and Welfare. (2022a). *Vital statistics.* Retrieved December 26, 2022, from https://view.officeapps.live.com/op/view.aspx?src=https%3A%2F%2Fwww.mhlw.go.jp%2Ftoukei%2Fsaikin%2Fhw%2Fjinkou%2Fkakutei21%2Fxls%2Fhyo.xlsx&wdOrigin=BROWSELINK

Ministry of Health, Labour and Welfare of Japan. (2022b). *Funds for business closure due to the COVID-19 response policies.* Retrieved January 3, 2023, from https://www.mhlw.go.jp/stf/kyugyoshienkin.html#gaiyou

Portal Site of Official Statistics of Japan. (2022). *Labour force survey/basic tabulation summary.* Retrieved December 28, 2022, from https://www.e-stat.go.jp/en/stat-search/files?page=1&query=unemployment%20rate&layout=dataset&stat_infid=000032230251

Statistic Korea. (2022a). *Marriage and divorce statistics in 2021.* Retrieved December 30, 2022a, from Marriage and Divorce http://kostat.go.kr/portal/eng/pressReleases/8/11/index.board?bmode=read&bSeq=&aSeq=417984&pageNo=1&rowNum=10&navCount=10&currPg=&searchInfo=&sTarget=title&sTxt=

Statistics Korea. (2022b). *Vital statistics of Korea.* Retrieved December 26, 2022b, from https://kosis.kr/statHtml/statHtml.do?orgId=101&tblId=DT_1B8000F&vw_cd=MT_ETITLE&list_id=A2_6&scrId=&language=en&seqNo=&lang_mode=en&obj_var_id=&itm_id=&conn_path=MT_ETITLE&path=%252Feng%252FstatisticsList%252FstatisticsListIndex.do

Strong, M. (2021). *Taiwan will only see lockdowns if 100 COVID cases per day over 14 days.* Retrieved December 29, 2022, from Taiwan News https://www.taiwannews.com.tw/en/news/4203920

Taiwan Centers for Disease Control. (2020). *Preparedness and contingency planning in response to COVID-19 epidemic.* Retrieved December 29, 2022, from COVID-19 coronavirus disease 2019 (COVID-19) https://www.cdc.gov.tw/En/File/Get/kccggG7ha69eNxZvZ4wyGw

Taiwan National Infectious Disease Statistics System. (2022). *Severe pneumonia with novel pathogens (COVID-19).* Retrieved December 30, 2022, from Taiwan National Infectious Disease Statistics System https://nidss.cdc.gov.tw/en/nndss/disease?id=19CoV

Taiwan News. (2021). *COVID vaccine deal with Taiwan falls through after Chinese pressure: Health minister*. Retrieved December 29, 2022, from Taiwan News https://www.taiwannews.com.tw/en/news/4129232

The Government of the Hong Kong Special Administrative Region. (2020). *Together, we fight the virus.* Retrieved December 29, 2022, from Fighting the Virus For Ten Months Sparing No Effort in Combating a Rebound and Achieving "Zero Infection" https://www.ceo.gov.hk/archive/5-term/eng/pdf/article20201127.pdf

Walker, K., & Thornton, J. (2016). Advanced maternal age. *Obstetrics, Gynaecology & Reproductive Medicine, 26*(12), 354–357. Retrieved December 28, 2022, from https://doi.org/10.1016/j.ogrm.2016.09.005

World Health Organization. (2020). *Archived: WHO Timeline—COVID-19.* Retrieved December 29, 2022, from World Health Organization https://www.who.int/news/item/27-04-2020-who-timeline---covid-19

World Health Organization. (2022). *WHO Coronavirus (COVID-19) dashboard*. Retrieved December 29, 2022, from World Health Organization https://covid19.who.int/data

Conclusion

Hirohisa Takenoshita

The COVID-19 pandemic started in 2020. In the initial period of the COVID-19 pandemic, we did not have any effective treatment or vaccines for the new coronavirus. In addition, there repeatedly emerged a new variant of COVID-19, thereby making it extremely difficult to prevent the spread of COVID-19. To curb the spread of this infectious disease, many countries introduced lockdown and social distancing measures. During the period of lockdown, schools and workplaces shut down, and many people were required to stay home. Such public health measures, however, had substantial influences on work and family lives in many parts of the world. This edited volume focused primarily on the impacts of the responses and policy measures to prevent the spread of COVID-19 on work and family lives in Japan and other Asian countries.

The first chapter discussed what determined access to home-based telework and its consequences for other domains in work and family lives in Japan. Due to the spread of COVID-19, the Japanese government requested private and public organizations to introduce telework to reduce face-to-face contact among people. Conversely, the author of this chapter found that access to telework differed markedly depending on education, employment contract, industry, and firm size. Thus, inequality in access to home-based telework would presumably contribute to increasing health inequality across individuals. Regarding the consequences of home-based telework, this chapter examined how home-based telework affected actual work hours, job satisfaction, and work-family conflicts. Although the introduction of home-based telework did not reduce actual working hours, it increased satisfaction with work hours among male workers. Meanwhile, the introduction of telework lowered the level of satisfaction among female workers. This finding may result from gender inequality in family responsibility. Even if women engage in paid work at home, they are also expected to do household chores. Home-based telework may probably increase the

H. Takenoshita (✉)
Keio University, Tokyo, Japan
e-mail: hirotake@law.keio.ac.jp

S. Matsuda and H. Takenoshita (eds.), *Changes in Work and Family Life in Japan Under COVID-19*, Population Studies of Japan, https://doi.org/10.1007/978-981-99-5850-4

psychological burden or stress of doing both paid work and housework. Based on this result, future studies need to consider how telework contributes to the reproduction or transformation of gender inequality in family and work spheres.

The second chapter also explored gender inequality in domestic work during the COVID-19 pandemic. The authors argued that the COVID-19 pandemic raised the demand for domestic work because of the expansion of home-based telework and the social distancing measure which required people to stay at home. Meanwhile, in Japan and other Asian countries, there was remarkable gender inequality in doing housework. Certainly, home-based telework enables married men to increase their time for housework. Exploring whether the gender gap in housework changed or not during the COVID-19 pandemic using the longitudinal survey data, this study found a slight decline in the gender gap in housework one year after the outbreak of the pandemic. The narrowing of this gender gap can be explained by the increased time availability for housework among men and relative resources and power for women. Conversely, this study found the persistence of gender inequality in family responsibilities, including housework and childcare, even after the pandemic. In addition, this study provided us with an interesting finding that there is a gender discrepancy in the perception of the husband's home-based telework. Husbands believe that they increase engagement in housework through working at home, whereas women feel more burdensome with their husbands' work at home.

In the third chapter, the authors considered how the policy measures that tackled the negative impact of COVID-19 on people's health affected fertility and pregnancy intention in Japan and other Asian countries. Interesting findings provided by this chapter are that the policy measures for the COVID-19 pandemic have led many people to postpone their marriage events, thereby contributing to declining fertility. Increased border control and restrictions on transnational movements also contributed to a decline in marriage between immigrants and natives in several Asian countries. According to the results of the survey data in Japan, some couples postponed their childbearing because there were increased restrictions on access to hospitals during the COVID-19 pandemic. In addition, as some couples were worried about the risk of infection for COVID-19 during the pregnancy period, they also postponed the child's pregnancy. Growing economic uncertainty during the COVID-19 pandemic also hindered couples from choosing to have more children in the future.

This edited volume tries to identify the impact of the COVID-19 policy measures on work and family lives from different perspectives: home-based telework, the gender gap in housework, and fertility behavior. The social distancing measure, which reduced face-to-face contact in our daily lives, had an enormous influence on work and family lives. The emergence of the new infectious disease produced a lot of challenges for us, but this challenge may also have some potential to change society or social structures in a good manner. For instance, home-based telework, which became more available to reduce face-to-face contact among employees, may increase job autonomy and flexibility in deciding when, where, and how long people work. Hence, the introduction of home-based telework may play a critical role in declining the conflict between work and family spheres.

Conversely, we should also account for how social inequality, which existed before the pandemic, is maintained or changed by this challenge. This book focused on inequality in access to telework, gender inequality in domestic work, and the role of economic inequality in shaping fertility behavior. The COVID-19 pandemic also highlights the fact that people who have economic disadvantages are more vulnerable to the pandemic. The impact of disasters on people's lives differs remarkably and depends on individuals' access to important resources. Policymakers and scholars should take the inequality perspective into account when disasters or any challenges occur in our society in the future. Future research also needs to consider how we can reduce inequality in access to resources and support from the government during the time of disasters or when a new infectious disease emerges in the future.

Acknowledgement
This study was made possible by funding from the Japan Society for the Promotion of Science. The Grant ID is 22H00917 and 18H00931. In the first and second chapters, we revised and updated the articles previously published in Sociological Theory and Methods, an official journal of the Japanese Association for Mathematical Sociology. We acknowledge the permission to use these two articles in different publications from the editorial board of Sociological Theory and Methods.

